ZEN
AND THE KINGDOM
OF HEAVEN

Reflections on the Tradition of Meditation
in Christianity and Zen Buddhism

ZEN

AND THE KINGDOM
OF HEAVEN

Tom Chetwynd

Wisdom Publications • Boston

Wisdom Publications
199 Elm St.
Somerville, MA 02144 USA
www.wisdompubs.org

Library of Congress Cataloging-in-Publication Data
Chetwynd, Tom.
    Zen and the kingdom of heaven: reflections on the tradition
of meditation in Christianity and Zen Buddhism/Tom Chetwynd.
        p. cm.
    Includes bibliographical references and index.
    ISBN 0-86171-187-4 (alk. paper)
    1. Meditation—Zen Buddhism. 2. Meditation—Catholic Church.
3. Zen Buddhism—Relations—Catholic Church. 4. Catholic
Church—Relations—Zen Buddhism.
    I. Title.
BQ9288 .C47 2000
291.4'35—dc21   00-049014

ISBN 0-86171-187-4

05 04 03 02 01
6   5   4   3   2

Design by Gopa & the Bear
Cover painting by Veetam

Wisdom Publications' books are printed on acid-free paper and meet
the guidelines for permanence and durability set by the Council on
Library Resources.

Printed in the United States of America

To the memory of Bridget and Diana

and all of the mothers before them

CONTENTS

PART TWO: *Christian Meditation in the Light of Zen*

ACKNOWLEDGMENTS

First and foremost I would like to thank Sochu Suzuki Roshi for the inspired way he got me to sit his *zazen* and try his *sesshin*. It was after that first seven-day retreat of Zen meditation that I began to understand something that had eluded me until then, namely the nature of Christian contemplative prayer (pure meditation without thought or image) that leads to the experience of the Kingdom of Heaven. But this most precious gift of his is not just for me: If this one ordinary Westerner can grasp his teaching, then so can anyone and everyone. He spared no effort on his visits to Europe and helped so many people. If it was Sochu Roshi who got me off to a quick burst at the beginning of this work (he was a sprinter like myself when young), it was Kyudo Roshi, his successor as abbot of Ryutakuji, who has provided much of the stamina to persevere in the long marathon since then. Both were marvelous at presenting only the essential point of Zen, so that what they offered was a truly universal spirituality. I am also grateful to Eizan Goto Roshi— as well as the younger monks, especially Ichiyo Hidemori Osho and Seimyo Maitani Osho, who stayed in London for two or three years—from whom I learned so much.

But it is entirely through Terence Griffin that I met any of these people. I cannot imagine anyone else who could have induced me to start practicing Zen. And ever since, his friendship has been invaluable. I do thank him from the bottom of my soul.

From there the trail of my debt winds back and forth. Terence himself first heard about Zen from a Benedictine monk, Dom Sebastian Moore. And throughout the years of my Zen practice, I am grateful for the continuous support of Father Jean Charles-Roux, who also introduced me to another very dear friend, Marion Stancioff. Marion alerted me to the importance of the *hesychast* controversy, as seen from the Eastern Orthodox view.

Kyudo Roshi once said: "Zen helps your life—but if you haven't got a life, it can't help." My wife, Hélène is my life as well as my love. But here I wish to thank her most especially for welcoming Sochu Roshi with open arms into our life, inviting him to stay in our home, thereby making it possible to share his wonderful friendship. Her warm, loving heart and intelligent, open mind have so helped Zen to flow smoothly with our Christian life together, and she has worked so hard to ensure this, much to the approval of Father Jean (her French chaplain in London). I was also much encouraged by my daughters, Yolanda and Bridget, who came to sit *sesshin* as soon as they were eligible at sixteen (and even came back for more). And I am grateful to all those who have helped me continue Sochu Roshi's work among Christians, especially Richard Garlick, Colin Rowbotham, and Judith Delevaux. I would also like to thank Sister Elaine MacInnes and her colleagues Kubota Roshi and Yamada Ryoun Roshi.

Among those who have hosted my Christian Zen group, I would like especially to thank Father Christopher Lowe, then Master of the Royal Foundation of St. Katherine's; the Reverend Donald Reeves of St. James' Picadilly; the Reverend Alan West of St. Alphege's; Sister Mercy Buckley of Fresh Horizons; the Reverend John Slater of St. John's Wood Church; the Reverend Roger Thacker of St. Paul's Hammersmith; and our very dear and helpful friend Sister Anne de Clerque of Holy Rood House (who had an inspiring visionary view of world religion). I am also grateful to Heythrop College, the International Quaker House, the Catholic Chaplaincy, and Patrice de Noblet for some special help.

But finally my gratitude must return to Sochu Roshi, one of the great Zen teachers of the twentieth century, and Kyudo Roshi, another remarkable teacher, both of whom are, for me, rather like the men that some of the Desert Fathers found standing by the door of their cave one night:

> [They] were strangers, whom no man knew, and they said concerning themselves that they had come from a far country. And they brought with them from that country many things of which the brethren had never heard and which existed not in the land of Egypt, that is to say, various kinds of fruit from Paradise.

INTRODUCTION

There used to be an Indian take-out place near my house, called "Curried-Away," which had the delightful idea of supplying a few books to go with the food. You could buy the books if you wanted or just read them while you were waiting for the food to be prepared. They were all on Sufism. "What a privilege it is for anyone to be born into one of the major world religions," I remember reading, "but what tragedy to die in it." This quotation stuck in my mind, though I was not quite sure what it meant at the time.

The story of world religion, when viewed as a whole, resembles the cosmic tree that grows upside down, its roots in the heavens and the stars. In the forest of d'Eawy in Normandy, I once saw a tree that grew to a great height as a single trunk, but, amazingly, one side of it seemed to be rough oak and the other half of the trunk smooth beech. It was known as the Lovers' Tree. In my mind, the image of the Lovers' Tree has become grafted into my image of the tree of world religion, with the ancient Hebrew religion and Hinduism as the twin trunks from which grew Christianity and Islam in Western Asia, and Buddhism in East Asia (with Taoism grafted in). Like most trees, the tree of world religion has only a few main branches and countless twigs—the numberless sects.

The Zen Buddhist sect and the Roman Catholic sect are like twigs at opposite ends of the tree. Zen stems from Chinese Buddhism, which in turn grew out of Hinduism. The twig of Zen is on the Mahayana branch of Buddhism. Mahayana Buddhism emphasizes the ideal of the bodhisattva, an enlightened being who refuses to rest until he or she has first helped every other living creature to attain enlightenment. The bodhisattva matures in wisdom and compassion together with all sentient beings. Mahayana Buddhism itself rubbed shoulders with Taoism for many centuries in China and absorbed much from this ancient source of Chinese wisdom before being taken to Japan. On this cosmic tree, what branches would possibly be farther apart than Zen Buddhism and Roman Catholicism?

Yet for me there was an enormous satisfaction in combining the two, in the very simple act of sitting facing the wall, not thinking—sitting in the manner of Asians, whether from the Near East or the Far East. If, to a Christian eye, it looks a little Oriental and peculiar when I sit cross-legged with no shoes or socks in a London church, that is because Christianity has become so thoroughly westernized over the course of many centuries. This posture certainly would not have looked at all strange to Christ himself—or to his first followers, who no doubt sat in very much the same manner. Nor would this posture appear strange to Eastern Orthodox Christians even to this day.

Just the simple act of a Christian meditating like this—doing *zazen* with a Buddhist teacher—seemed to me to manifest unity within the great diversity of traditions. My teachers were from the other side of the world, and from the most eastern branch of the tree of world religion. Sometimes, of course, differences showed through clearly. But that was only superficial—underneath, my Zen teachers were like spiritual fathers who continued to care for and challenge me, however difficult I might have been at times.

The only requirement my teachers had for me was that I practice *zazen* in the recognized—and effective—way. There is only one way to do *zazen*.

Apart from that, I didn't need to change my beliefs at all. Zen does not require uniform thinking, or behavior, or living. My Zen teachers were delighted to nurture every aspect of my Christian life.

Thus have I come to understand that saying from the Sufi book in Curried-Away: I had had the privilege to be born into Christianity, but because I had encountered Zen, I would not die in it—I would *live* in it.

PART ONE

Zen Experience

When you hear me talk about the void,

do not at once fall into the idea of vacuity.

Hui Neng, Sixth Zen Patriarch (638–713)

1 THE FIRST STEP

Difficulty at the Beginning

W hen I first started sitting in Zen meditation, the experience was uncomfortable and boring. Very often the thought came at me with great force that this was an imbecilic waste of time. Many people who have tried Zen meditation have felt that same urge to throw up their arms and walk out. It seemed impossible to believe that anything good could come of it. You start sitting facing the wall and you end up sitting facing the wall. Where on earth could it lead? I have described this overwhelming feeling of futility in some detail, because it is probably the first great barrier that each of us will have to overcome if we are ever going to re-establish meditation as the core Christian practice that it once was.

It is more than likely when you first start to practice, that you will walk into a room of people more experienced than yourself. The temptation is to rapidly conclude that perhaps meditation is all right for some—since they have continued to do it, they must be getting something out of it—but dead wrong for you. In my case, meditation started out painful and tedious beyond words. Extremely convincing arguments for giving up before you have even started will almost certainly occur to you—don't listen to them.

If you have started at all, there were probably reasons for it—try to remember what they were. For me, the atmosphere created by the practice of others helped. And there was a glimmer of hope that there was some goal to be attained this way—that there was an inner spiritual ladder that would lead to the star of my destiny, and not just worn-out stairs leading to endless boredom and frustration.

The most important thing, I realized, is that Zen sitting has much in common with learning a sport, or learning to read, for that matter. It is tedious and frustrating at first, but years of enjoyment lie ahead once you have mastered it.

But, also like reading and like sports, with a good teacher, and determined practice, one's experience of the process begins to change and things start to look very different, sometimes even quite quickly.

Just Sitting Facing the Wall

I had never sat in Zen meditation before, but I had heard that a Zen Buddhist monk was due to arrive from Japan in a few weeks at an apartment within walking distance of where I lived. I'd heard about his previous visits, but for some reason it seemed important—imperative—that *this* time I go and have a look at him. But before he got here, I would have to learn a little bit about Zen.

My friend Terence and I climbed the stairs to the where the Zen meditation group usually practiced. The echo in the staircase seemed to amplify the nervous apprehension we both felt. But the apprehension was only on the surface. Underneath it we both felt a deep flow of excitement. Flat number seven, the flat the Zen group used for meditation, was on the top floor. Seven steps up a ziggurat to contemplate the seven stars of the Great Bear pointing to the Pole Star—could this be the linoleum-covered staircase to heaven?

Terence battled with the sliding door above me, but it wouldn't open. And the key wasn't under the mat. We sat on the stairs for a while in case somebody appeared with the key, but nobody did. So we left, ostensibly relieved.

The plan had been that Terence would show me the posture and the breathing for Zen sitting, then we would sit for two hours and go off and have a drink. Since we couldn't get in, we ended up having a cup of tea together in a café, and he talked about his Zen experiences. As we talked, it was as if the teacup in front of him were the only thing ever created and it existed by itself in an endless void. The teacup shone magnificently for that moment, alone in empty space.

On another night I returned without Terence to that flat, got past the sliding door, took off my shoes and entered the room where the London group meditated. It felt like entering a holy place. Like Moses, I had taken off my shoes before treading on holy ground. It was a familiar feeling, but it seemed as if I had been deprived of it for a long time, and I was glad to be in that room just then.

The same feeling had swept over me most often as a child as I entered the quiet little chapel set aside for the new boys at the Benedictine prep school I'd attended, or as I knelt down to pray in front of the school's special statue of Our Lady. Years later, I had felt that same feeling again as I entered the gates of a convent in Suffolk and was overcome with a sense of awe.

I piled up the cushions on a mat and tried to arrange my large stiff legs around them. It wasn't that I was getting stiffer with age. My rigid little mind had inhabited a stiff little body even when I was a boy. I could never touch my toes or sit cross-legged comfortably. At the age of thirty-six, I was probably about as supple as I'd ever been.

A European fellow, looking like a medieval monk prematurely aged with ascetic discipline, came over and gave me what was clearly the wrong advice. He advised me to use fewer cushions. Nobody could sit properly with so many cushions, he said—so he took two away, leaving me without nearly enough cushions. I showed him that my knees weren't touching the floor. He whispered that it didn't matter, my knees would sink slowly onto the floor—but I knew they never would.

The fellow in charge banged the clappers and rang the bell for sitting to begin, and I sat there facing the wall, very uncomfortable, with my knees in the air, my body bent forward so as not to topple over backward. I tried to concentrate on counting my outgoing breaths, a practice that was supposed to drive out all thoughts.

Onnnnnnne... That damn fool, I thought.

Twooooooo... Why on earth did I take any notice of him?

Threeeeeeee... Terence had told me to get my knees on the floor at all costs, to form a solid tripod.

Two hours eventually passed, and I was glad to get away.

I had variations of this experience frequently in the remaining days before the monk's arrival. I became increasingly familiar with the difficulties of sitting facing a wall, doing *zazen*. I spend a good deal of time in flat number seven trying to count my breath. Bells were rung and clappers were clapped, and we got up and walked around doing *kinhin* (walking meditation). Then I'd sit down again with another struggle, heaving my legs into place like logs that don't quite fit into the fireplace. There I'd sit—feeling pain in the knees and counting the breath mechanically, pointlessly. What *was* the point of it all?

Terence had lent me some leaflets written by Katsuki Sekida, which were later compiled into the book, *Zen Training*. The point seemed simple: don't think. But that turned out to not be so easy—

Onnnnnnne...

The Cloud of Unknowing, a book by a fourteenth-century Christian monk, mentions that you're supposed to concentrate on a short word such as "God" or "sin." But don't think about that now—

Twooooooo...

Let go of all thoughts. Just breathe. Just sit. I must not think about the instructions for sitting while sitting. I must get a clear idea in my head beforehand, and then just sit. Just breathe. The breath of life. Is it *ruach* in Hebrew, the symbol of the spirit? Three years studying theology, and all for nothing. And now all this for the sake of a Japanese monk. Of course he was bound to be a disappointment. What was he doing coming to London anyway, instead of staying in his monastery where he belonged? Perhaps he wasn't wanted there. Some sort of charlatan.

Why don't I just get up and go—and never come back. The pain in the knees is intolerable! Why doesn't *everybody* just get up and go? None of them look the athletic type exactly. Yet they are all sitting so quietly, in this holy place. What have they got that I haven't?

I feel like rolling on my back, kicking my legs in the air and screaming.... Why don't I?

But I was on the school boxing team, and the rugby team. I should be able to handle this. Sure, it was years ago that I played rugby... all the same I should be able to sit facing a wall. Anyway, here's my chance to prove I'm made of that caliber—

Onnnnnnne....

Then, during one of these interminable sittings, a wonderful thing happened—the pain was suddenly gone! This was just what the leaflets said would happen! But then, right when I was managing to sit there feeling relaxed for the first time since I'd started, *ting* went the bell to end the period. My legs had gone quite dead. I crawled around on all fours as I put my mat and cushions against the wall. I clambered upright keeping close to the wall, squeezing and shaking my buttocks, trying to bring sensation back. I stayed propped against the wall until the person next to me came around a second time, and I moved off after him.

Then it was time to sit down again. Unfortunately, I didn't get my cushions quite right. I kept feeling as if I were about to topple into the person next to me. I imagined we'd all fall down like bowling pins. And now the pain was getting worse by the minute.

It must be time for the bell to ring. Come on, ring the bell! A little movement came from the direction of the timekeeper—he must be reaching for the bell to end the period! But he wasn't.

In that moment, I decided Zen really wasn't for me. But the Japanese monk would be here the next day, and after all the struggle that I'd been through, I figured I may as well set eyes on him at least. But this was definitely not for me.

It was different for Terence. He was fascinated by everything Japanese—martial arts, calligraphy, haiku. But I knew practically nothing about any of it and didn't care much either.

On the other hand, I was fascinated by Christianity. Terence wasn't. For years we talked about everything under the sun except Christianity, which was a total blank to him, even though we had spent ten years at the same boarding school run by Benedictine monks. After leaving school, he went to Oxford for a term or two, and then returned to London and stayed in his room for six months, getting his mother to keep him supplied with books from the public library. He was extremely well-read.

But then all of a sudden, Terence started asking questions about Christianity. He had started practicing Zen and had come across books comparing it with Christianity, such as D.T. Suzuki's comparative study of certain Zen masters and Meister Eckhart. He got me interested in Zen through books like Blythe's *Zen in English Literature*. Like many Western people, if I thought of Buddhists at all, I thought of them as nihilists striving to attain some calm, empty state of *nirvana* even more boring than the usual run of utopias and heavens that man has devised. But such objections to Buddhism had already been refuted by Hui Neng, the sixth Zen patriarch, more than a thousand years ago. He pointed out that monks would not devote themselves night and day, body and soul, in order to attain nihilism. His contemporaries in China were already accusing the Buddhist monks of being nihilists, whereas in fact they were striving for the highest reality accessible to humankind.

So, through Terence, I was beginning to learn a little about the Zen tradition and its lineage of great masters. But none of this inspired any confidence in the Japanese monk who was coming to London.

After all, there had been great men in Christianity's past too. But now it stood like a ruin of its former self, with crumbling pillars and fallen rafters. And this had left room for a lot of fringe religious groups to move in and camp on the abandoned sites. Let them forage for spiritual food as best they could—they could count me out of the wild goose chase.

I made up my mind to take one look at the monk tomorrow and then get out of there. I wasn't easily hoodwinked. One hard look and I'd know.

The Zen Monk Arrives

On the day the monk was to arrive, I felt fear mixed with excitement—but I was already preparing my usual defenses against another disappointment.

As I entered the Zen group's flat, to my surprise the newly-arrived monk was crossing the hall. Our eyes met. Natural enough. But something in me leaped for joy involuntarily. Of course this meeting in the hall was just a coincidence—but I remembered a fragment of a story Terence had told me: A thousand years ago on the mountainous plateau of Tibet, the great sage Marpa had pretended to be busy in a field so as to be out there to greet Milarepa, the man who would be his disciple, when he arrived.

The other times I'd come to this flat, there were few enough people here that I could grab two or three cushions for myself. But now there were so many people that there were too few cushions to go around. So my knees were stuck in the air again, and I had difficulty getting my back straight. Yet oddly, it was somehow easier sitting with the monk in the room. I came back to sit with the monk frequently.

One evening I was sitting on the window side of the room with the sweat pouring off me. The monk got up and stood just behind my left shoulder—perhaps he thought the amount I sweated was related to the amount I drank—yet his presence behind me was only reassuring. At the end, after we'd chanted and bowed, he said a few words about Zen sitting: "*Zazen*—body laundry," he said, making gestures as if he were a washing machine with the clothes going around and around in his stomach. It was true, my mind felt clean, pure—like a fresh shirt back from the laundry.

Another evening during meditation, I must have dozed off into a half-dream. The wall in front of me dissolved, and I was confronted by three wolves! I still knew where I was—in that room with the monk behind me—but the wolves were real, too, and menacing. I recognized them. They were the same three wolves that had followed me when I was seventeen, hitchhiking near the border of Yugoslavia. The ground had been covered in snow and ice that February night, and the wolves started howling as they came toward me over the snow from a distant copse. They had followed me. In my half-dream, I was aware that these wolves were only vivid memories, figments of my mind, yet they seemed to embody very real vicious forces that could still tear me apart now. From behind me the monk gave clear instructions: "Say *Mmmmuuuuu*, loud, to reach the sea." I did so, loud enough to blast away the wall, let alone the wolves. When they were gone I found myself still saying, "*Mmmmuuuuu...*" out loud, but all by myself. The rest of the room was silent, so I trailed off into silence myself. I never quite made up my mind whether the monk had really given those instructions, or whether I just had heard him in my head, vivid as the wolves.

There had certainly been a strange atmosphere in that room since the monk had arrived, a feeling of crossing borders into untrodden lands—far stranger than being turned out of a truck in the middle of the night near the border of wolf-infested Yugoslavia.

After I had been going to sit with the monk in the evenings for about a week, I woke up early one morning very alert, with just enough time to get to the flat and sit with the monk for the two hours before dawn. After the sitting, as I stepped out of the building, dawn was breaking over London on a bright cold winter's day.

I felt very pure, refreshed. I had not felt quite like that since I was a child. It reminded me of going to serve Mass as an altar boy in the early morning during the school holidays.

When I first heard of Terence getting up at 5:30 A.M. to go to Zen sitting, I thought he was completely mad. But after that morning's experience, I started going in the mornings as well as the evenings—but just while the monk was there. He was by no means my ideal image of a monk. He wasn't at all ethereal or spiritual looking. He was earthy and bouncy. It was hard to figure out what impressed me about him, why I liked him. I just did. And next to the real monk my ideal image paled. But that image was a holdover from my childhood ideas about monks, easily discarded in the face of this man who was real, the living embodiment of the spiritual life.

But I continued to have problems during meditation with my legs. Anybody who has tried Zen sitting, even for half an hour, will know something about the problem of the legs. Everybody thinks that his particular pair of legs is especially unsuited to sitting in that position. First the pain becomes excruciating. Then the legs go numb.

Once, when the sitting period ended, I was too vain to crawl around and clutch at the wall in front of the monk—so instead I stood up abruptly and crashed to the floor immediately.

"Stand up. Quiet!" said the monk ferociously.

I had twisted my ankle, so I hobbled around the room in pain. It was one of the worst sittings so far. I reflected that on top of everything else, we had to pay dues to cover the monk's airfares from Japan.

I left in a glum, resentful mood, and remembered telling my daughter, Bridget, about the stigmata. "That's wonderful," she said. "You mean you try to do everything you can to please God, and then in return he goes and gives you these big holes in your hands that keep bleeding. Thank you very much God, just what I always wanted."

Eventually, though, I had a remarkable *positive* Zen experience—and the monk took full advantage of it. I was sitting near the monk and had managed to achieve a state of comparative inner quiet, like a calm grey light—first light just before the dawn. Then it dawned on me: *I am*.

It was so simple. Yet it was more exciting than daybreak over London on a clear, crisp morning. It was a warm, delicious feeling and I basked in it, like someone lying on a beach with great waves from the Atlantic breaking somewhere beyond his feet. When I got up to walk around, I was surprised to find that my legs were neither painful nor numb. When I sat down again, it was still just as true: *I am*. The same delicious feeling broke over me again and continued to surge through me. It came in waves. When one wave trembled to its end and was beginning to slide away, another took its place, from an endless ocean. *I am*, life from life.

After the sitting we turned toward the center of the room as usual to chant unfamiliar Buddhist chants. Then the monk sometimes said a few words. He looked directly at me and said, "You are like a baby." He made himself look like a baby, pursing his lips and sucking his thumb as if it were a bottle. "Tasting, tasting."

I understood that I had had a first taste of Zen experience. He was no longer looking at me, but I felt that it was still meant for me when he said, "Now *sesshin*. Okay to leave wife. More sitting. Come."

Sesshin was the Zen retreat about to start. It was a whole week away in the country, and I had decided not to go. But his words reminded me of Christ's words about leaving your wife and your family to follow him. The monk didn't know that I was married, or that I was a Christian, so I couldn't help but wonder if perhaps the Holy Spirit was inviting me to attend this Zen retreat—through the mouth of this Japanese Buddhist monk. I looked at him hard. It was by no means impossible that the Holy Spirit could have a foothold in such a man, even though he wasn't Christian.

The last time I had been on a retreat was at school with the Benedictine monks. Neither of my parents were Catholics, nor was my elder brother, but I was sent to a Catholic school at the age of eight because I was already so interested in Christianity. Since then, I had spent more than a quarter of a century trying to get some taste of the spiritual food, but it was as if the taste had been fading away each year. And now, suddenly, in a mere two weeks of sitting facing a wall, it had dawned on me that I am. A realization that was interwoven with the crux of my faith, by association with the God who said "I am who I am," and Christ, who said, "Before Abraham was, I am."

I thought about that chance encounter on the landing when the monk's eyes met mine for a moment—such a small coincidence, his passing at the very moment I slid open the door. I thought again about the meeting of the sage Marpa and his great disciple Milarepa. But the important events in history—just because they happened hundreds of years ago, thousands of miles away, and above all to somebody else—pale into insignificance beside comparatively trifling incidents if they should happen to you personally, here and now.

Another factor urged me to go on this *sesshin*: it was Lent, the traditional time for Christians to fast and to pray and to go on retreats. It was the season of forty days that commemorated the time Christ spent meditating in the desert before angels came and ministered to him, and the forty years Moses led his people in the wilderness before they entered the promised land.

I decided I had to go.

Difficulties presented themselves.

It wasn't as if I were being asked to give up everything. I could spare one week of my life, I thought.

More difficulties presented themselves until I felt as if I were rowing a fragile boat through a narrow defile before the great rocks to either side crashed together, crushing me and my spiritual boat forever.

What if this is the opportunity for which I've been waiting for such a long time? I could spend the rest of my life waiting for just this opportunity—which I would have already missed.

Finally, I made up my mind. I told my wife, Hélène, that I intended to go. She objected strenuously. What on earth was I getting myself into? For her, even more than for me, "fringe" religious groups were highly suspect. But then she had not set eyes on this particular monk. I said I was sorry, but I had to go.

My First Zen Retreat

We loaded Buddha statues, gongs, chant books, Zen cushions, Zen mats, as well as plenty of rice, into the waiting cars. On the way up and down the stairs, Michael (the gaunt figure who had taken away two of my cushions the first time I sat with the London Zen group) had plenty of time to warn me that it was very unwise to try to do a seven-day *sesshin* straight off with so little preparation. We would be sitting ten hours a day. "The sitting will be very hard," he advised me, "even for someone much more experienced and properly prepared." I do not believe in reincarnation, but I would not have been a bit surprised to learn that some remote uncle of his, looking exactly like him, had been the bursar in a medieval monastery.

If he can do it so can I, I thought.

I walked down the linoleum-covered stairs with the last load of supplies, got into the car, and drove away—with all the threads that connected me to my usual everyday life snapping behind me.

We arrived at a comfortable house in the country, quickly stripped the sitting room bare of furniture, arranged a small altar in the bay window, and laid out mats and cushions. Instinctively I grabbed a position near the monk and the altar, in a secure corner where the wall jutted out just before the window recess, so the monk was directly behind my shoulder. He faced inward, whereas the rest of us faced the wall. Another Japanese person had come to the retreat, which I thought augured well—as when you find Chinese people eating in a Chinese restaurant. We sat for an hour that evening, and by the end of it, the room seemed transformed into a sacred precinct, a holy place.

Early the next morning the sitting began in earnest. It was terrible. The worst ordeal of my life. Death will surely be like falling off a log after that. Just one week, I kept reminding myself. Just this once, and never again.

I started by blaming myself for my misery. I had stupidly twisted my ankle and that didn't help. I had the wrong body for it anyway. I was too old to learn new tricks. I was the wrong sort of person for this.

Then with the pain in my knees mounting, with my ankle swelling, my back aching, and time dragging interminably, I soon moved on to blaming the monk. It became increasingly obvious that he was an undesirable in Japan, desperately trying to get a group together here to support him in his old age. The other Japanese man was probably in conspiracy with him. They were a couple of clever charlatans who had managed to hoodwink all these suckers— but how? Why on earth were all these people here?

Try, I told myself. Don't waste time. Just this one week. I know that if I don't get through this week, I'll just make myself come back and try again. And it'll be even worse next time. Some of the other people in the room look so wimpy. How can they stand it? I must not let them have the satisfaction of seeing me give up. Especially not Michael.

People work from 9 A.M. to 5 P.M. just to get by and maintain the status quo. Once I had thought that if anyone did that for the sake of spiritual treasure, they might get somewhere important. And here we are sitting from 5 A.M. to 9 P.M. My big chance. Try again. Try to find the empty space inside where the pain won't reach. Concentrate—

Onnnnnnne… concentrate on the lower belly.

The trouble with concentrating your energy in the lower belly is that it is right next to the place where the pain was coming from.

But after a while I worked out rather a clever system. I pretended I was a doll with a lot of strings inside me, strings that went from the lower stomach up to the head and from there back down to the various limbs including the painful hips and knees. Then I would snip the strings just above the stomach at the same time that I thrust all my energy into the lower belly, letting the air out like a jet.

Twooooooo...

At last I was free of limbs for a while, alert yet empty. And from that pure clear state came another phrase from the Gospels: "Out of your bellies will flow fountains of living water." It was not like a dream or a hallucination. It was just the plain actual words, spoken two thousand years ago and reaching me right then, pristine and meaningful—encouraging words for my particular circumstances. And all was well for a while.

Some sittings went better than others. I began to recognize the signs, as I settled down, of whether my knees were going to act up or not. If it wasn't the knees, it could be the thighs: I felt as if I were being forced to do the splits. Or else it was my ankle throbbing painfully. One evening I consulted the monk about it. He just said: "More sitting. Strong sitting." In that instant I could not help admiring him. Something convinced me that he was concerned about me—yet he could be so harsh. I didn't remember ever having encountered such a fierce kind of concern before.

But the next day I was soon back to wondering how on earth I could have given him the benefit of my very considerable doubts. Toward the end of a bad sitting I sometimes fell back on my imagination as a last resort. It was not Zen sitting, but it was my last-ditch stand. It was either do that or give up. I would pretend that I was in an iron cage with sharp spikes a millimeter from my eyeballs and face. If I moved so much as a millimeter, my eyeballs would be pierced, my face torn to shreds. The fantasy was particularly effective because I had recently had a nightmare in which my face had been badly stitched up in a repulsive patchwork of skin that twisted in a spiral.

"Surely it's about time to ring that bell. It must be time to ring the bell. Ring that bell!" I would scream inside my head. Yet somehow it would never ring until I was calm and settled-in for more strong sitting.

The bell released us for a brief walk-around, or for chanting, and occasionally for a meal followed by a work period. During the meals I would lean against the wall like a sack of old potatoes, utterly exhausted. The tea was a godsend. Unlike everybody else at the retreat, I used the big bowl for tea and the little ones for the rice. Rice gives me constipation. Even the monk seemed suspicious of this particularly nasty brown rice: he advised chewing each mouthful a hundred times. Then the tea came around again for washing out the bowls.

Each morning, during the work period, I worked in the garden.

Each afternoon the monk gave a talk, his *teisho*. The other Japanese man attempted to translate. There was a burst of Japanese talk, followed by a slow, incomprehensible translation, punctuated with a few excited but disjointed words from the monk's limited English vocabulary, plus a certain amount of banging on the floor. It all made me feel extremely sleepy.

The monk started talking about a cart. Through the translator, he said, "Take off wheels. What is it?" I roused myself from my torpor and suggested, "a broken down old cart?" Everybody laughed except the monk, who was quite cross. Through his interpreter he tried to explain the deep spiritual significance of this Zen riddle, called a *koan* (pronounced *ko-an*), but I rather doubted that anybody got the point.

Another day he mentioned that he had been in a prisoner-of-war camp during World War II. Later it occurred to me that he was putting us through all this torture just to get even with us.

Suddenly on the third day he broke off his talk and announced, "Tea!" I was afraid he must have noticed me nodding off, but I was always glad to have some tea. He returned from the kitchen with an enormous pudding basin and various other things. In it he mixed up a vicious-looking bright green concoction and announced with obvious satisfaction, "Tea drinking: open eyes."

Until then, the suspicious side of my nature had been baffled by what was going on. How had this monk managed to lure these people into sitting facing the wall, in agony for hours on end, and make them pay money for it? Now if we drank this bilious-looking green stuff, our eyes would suddenly open. I had had a good dose of mescaline once, and knew what it could do. A strong brew of "grass"—or whatever this was—and we would all go away quite satisfied with our wonderful experience. Three days of strenuous effort would make us particularly susceptible. So when my turn came, I kept my lips tightly shut and just let a little bit of the stuff touch them, so as to taste it. The others took great gulps from the bowl. I had to admit the brew smelled and tasted harmless enough.

The house in which the retreat took place was an old rectory. And at the end of the day I went out for a stroll and slipped into the fine Anglican church next door. It was so quiet and empty with the sanctuary lamp burning. I was happy to pray there, on my knees, for a while. And as I did so my head began to clear. For the first time it seemed definite that I had been led to come on this retreat by my own angels and not by demonic powers. The monk was obviously a pure and saintly man who had come a long way to try to teach me something. And he served tea when I looked sleepy—odd Japanese tea perhaps, but nobody had looked "high" or behaved strangely after it. Just another morning and I'd be halfway through the retreat.

Again a voice came from the past: "Don't become a laughing-stock, like the man who built half a tower then found he could not complete it. And if your armies are only half the strength of the enemy, then don't engage in the battle."

I stared around the church as if half expecting to see the figure who'd spoken those words so long ago. Looking up into the great

Gothic rib cage of the church, I was reminded of the three days Jonah spent in the belly of the whale, and how at the end of the third day he was cast up on the beach. I felt a bit like that today, at the end of the third day of being confined to my mat.

I made up my mind to sit with vigor during the remaining four days of the retreat.

Outside the church it was cold. Clouds were gathering and only one star was visible.

At night we each slept on the same patch of floor upon which we had sat during the day. With the mat under me and the cushion for a pillow, it was a relief to stretch out in my sleeping bag. I fell asleep instantly.

I woke fresh and alert, with a pure feeling inside. Outside it had snowed during the night.

My first thought on waking was that I had found a real retreat, carried out in pure silence. I imagined that if I were in some remote hermitage in the mountains, or in a grand medieval monastery like Lindisfarne, on an island cut off by the spring tides, it would not be so very different—just practicing the prayer of quiet in Lent, pure contemplative prayer. I felt at home, part of a great living tradition that had always connected the Spirit of Truth with the breath of life: just breathing. And the Holy Spirit had the reputation of moving where it liked, like the wind outside—the mad March gales.

The monk took us outside for some brisk exercises before sitting. It was still dark, and the light from the room shone out across the snow.

Two and a half hours before breakfast and the first cup of tea—and not a moment to be wasted. I did not want to put Hélène through all her anxiety—and myself through all this agony—for nothing. Today, my legs folded under me comparatively easily. And when I got up to walk around, I was light and agile—more agile than I'd felt for years. The agility did not last, but my determination did not waver again. I had scented the elusive quarry, and my heart was in full cry after it. At last the tea was passed and poured, and a steaming bowl was now in front of me. The bowl was at my lips and the first delicious gulp was down before I remembered where I was. More than twenty people were lined around the walls, waiting until everyone was served, waiting for the monk to give the signal for breakfast to start. I put my bowl down—embarrassed—but to my surprise the monk smiled at me warmly.

I heard the wind outside. I have always loved the wind. Soon I would be out in the garden, digging the beds, turning the earth.

Never had the daffodils shone so brightly as they did that morning. I had drawn many pictures of daffodils as a boy and had a particular soft spot for them. But it wasn't just the daffodils that gleamed against the snow this morning during the work period—the earth glistened as I turned it. I had never before noticed how the rich color and texture of the earth are like a jewel—but a jewel that provides us with food and flowers.

The wind and the earth, the daffodils and the snow—now I noticed them, as if appreciating them for the first time. After three days of sitting, I seemed to be getting more on the monk's wavelength. And, more strikingly, he seemed to have found my wavelength.

Glancing at me out of the corner of his eye, he started his talk that afternoon: "You think Japanese monk talk nonsense." It was as if he'd picked the thought out of my head at his last talk, though it was probably written all over my face. "Not nonsense," he said. Then a burst of Japanese apparently to the effect that the words would come back to us later and mean something at the appropriate time. Again I had an image of Christ telling his apostles that even if they didn't understand what he was saying now, they would when the Spirit of Truth had led them into revelation.

Then he began talking about "one mind"—as if he also thought we were getting onto each other's wavelength. "Everyone same. Eyes, nose—same. Mind, too—same mind. One mind." As if human society, forming the single body of Christ, were a vivid reality to this Buddhist monk.

He unwrapped his book of *koans*, which he kept tied up in a piece of cloth. (He'd arrived at the retreat with all his belongings and bedding in a huge piece of cloth, just as if he had once set out from Japan with it all tied on the end of a pole.) Today's story was about a fellow called Zuigan who talked to himself. Every morning Zuigan would say: "Zuigan, are you there?" "Yes, Master," he'd reply to himself. "Don't be deceived by anyone." "No, I won't."

"Who master? Where master?" The monk before me thumped his lower belly, "Here."

It was all a bit zany, but rather delightful. He often ended his talk saying, "Too much talk. No good. More sitting."

The following morning I woke up longing to get started. It was as if the day before had been that necessary easing up along the back straight of a 440-yard race. And now just two more days. I hoped that I could muster a solid final burst along the home stretch.

Again we exercised outside, where the snow had melted and the warm wind was whirling in circles. When we came back inside, we began to sit again, strenuously.

It occurred to me that this wasn't unlike trying to defecate when you were constipated—a stray thought, let go of it.

Then I imagined my head had been lopped off and rolled way down the garden path. My body followed, rolling away from me, slice by slice, like misshapen wheels, rolling over the horizon. No rut, no wheels—the cart was no longer a cart. I recalled the monk's question from the day before.

It was as if there were no one left on the cushion. Nobody on the mat. Nothing to divide my breath from the wind outside. So free. Then the wind and breath dissolved.

It was as if the monk knew what had happened. He announced that anyone who wished to remain seated could do so, then rang his bell. While the others walked around behind me, I remained secure in my corner. But not confined there. I was no longer the prisoner of my body. I had broken loose from my own rib cage. I had burst through the mind's barriers. Behind me the others settled down again. Now or never. I pressed on—I didn't know where. Without desire, without goal. Then it was time for breakfast.

After breakfast it was my turn to do the washing up. The monk came into the kitchen just as the people in charge of cooking were about to throw away some orange peels and cauliflower stalks. "Don't waste. Best part," he said. He would cook them. He drove the others out of the kitchen. He chopped up orange peels and cauliflower stalks behind me, while I washed the dishes meticulously, delighting in the splashing water. The monk kept popping an extra spoon or knife into the sink for me to wash. Why had it so infuriated me when my father had done the same thing years before? I cleaned the stove and left the sink resplendent, as if it were in my nature to be so meticulous. Everything in the kitchen shone with its own bright existence. And outside, it was the same. Some of the daffodils had been broken by the winds, so I picked them and put them in a gleaming milk bottle in the kitchen.

There wasn't time to start gardening, so I went back to my mat. There were already two other people sitting. A great urgency was driving through me, driving me on, but I wasn't expecting anything. I just wanted to sit, now that I'd discovered how to do it. It was as if I had been deprived of sitting all of my life. I was beginning to realize that sitting was the one sure and calculated way of restoring the soul to its natural state of grace.

Very quickly I dismantled myself like the cart. I disintegrated; I dissolved. I was aware of people coming in quietly, arranging themselves on their cushions. Clappers and bells sounded for the next period of sitting, but it was as if my own place were empty. Time passed quickly. Bells and clappers sounded again and people walked around. While they were doing so, I became aware that I was sitting—but only as if I were an outline on the mat that quickly dissolved again as soon as they settled down.

My breath was very fine. Above the turbulent winds, the air was very still. Silence, stillness, peace. The air was becoming more and more rarefied. For hours that day, and for days before that, I had been gradually melting into this still rarefied state—and suddenly I was bored. Bored by the silent empty spaces, vast empty reaches of the mind that stretched beyond the edges of the universe.

I had been completely dismantled. How would I find the parts and reassemble the person, just one person among the teeming millions of people on earth? I don't know whether it took any time or not, absorbing this situation, but all of a sudden I was back on my mat, with Daryl the Jewish Doctor beside me, in a country rectory with a Japanese monk. I was focused on this particular place in an unlimited universe, at this particular moment, the culmination of millions of years. Just ordinary everyday life, the same as it was before I came on retreat: the kitchen, the garden, here and at home, unchanged, except that my body was shaken with tears that were splashing onto my hands. I didn't want to disturb the others, but it couldn't be helped. It was as if I had suddenly caught a glimpse of my own life, just as it was, but seen in its proper context, put back in its right perspective at last—as if I had been missing it up until then, failing to appreciate it properly.

By lunchtime I was completely drained and ravenously hungry. Zen sitting was surprisingly strenuous. When I got home I discovered I had lost fourteen pounds on that retreat. Meanwhile the beans, orange peels, and cauliflower stalks were indeed quite delicious. And after lunch the garden was more beautiful than ever. The weather had changed and spring was breaking loose, but it was as mild and warm as early summer. It was as if all four seasons—a whole year—had been packed into those few days.

When I went for my private interview, the room was dimly lit and the monk seemed to glow radiantly in the dark. I tried to describe my experience before lunch, and as I did so happiness and gratitude flooded through me again. The translator could not conceal his excitement. The monk seemed pleased, but noncommittal.

Later that evening I was summoned back to the monk's room, but he was alone this time. There was more light, yet his body still glowed. He had become very eloquent with his gestures and his few English words. We got on easily. In London, I had sipped at Zen like a baby at a bottle, now I was gulping it down like tea from the huge pudding basin. I felt as if I were taking a vast draught of exquisitely clear, pure water after having been parched in the desert for all of my life."Universe drinking," the monk said to me. My experience was so difficult to describe, so elusive—but he knew. He knew what I had experienced, and I was very lucky. He had nothing more to give me. I thanked him very much.

The next day we piled Buddha statues, gongs, mats, and cushions into cars and sped along the roads back to London and home. I felt so free, liberated from the iron cage with spikes—I need never do another Zen retreat ever again!

For all my reading, I had never imagined anything like that Zen retreat. It was completely new to me that meditation could be so intense, so calculated, and so effective. Sitting in a group, the stillness, the calm breathing, the position of the eyes, the hands, the timing (half-hour bursts of meditation having a cumulative effect over three days), the breakthrough, and then another three days, all the details calculated to make a profound psychological change, to effect a deep inner transformation.

It had given me a completely new outlook on life. I realized that all of us are in danger of missing our own lives, failing to appreciate our own living experience. To change this, there are two stages involved. First, one must turn away from ordinary living in order to contact the life-process at the point where it is closest and most intimate, ourselves; just sitting facing the wall, hour after hour, day after day, until the truth manifested. Then second, one returns to ordinary extroverted life—which is now no longer so ordinary.

In the last few centuries, Christians had been trying to leave out the important—but extremely difficult—first stage. It wasn't always so. I already knew something about the arduous spiritual training of the early Christians, enough to realize that it may have been a bit like Zen, calculated to have the same effect. I would investigate further.

Nevertheless the main point wasn't hearing about it or reading about it, but seeking it out and experiencing it firsthand. I realized now how immensely important the role of teacher was: he was the proof, the living demonstration of the value of what he did—and what he did was *zazen*.

2 BABY ZENDO AND SOCHU ROSHI

After six years of hard ascetic discipline, Shakyamuni Buddha indulged in a bowl of bean curd, which gave his emaciated frame the energy to sit strongly through the night, and he was enlightened when he saw the morning star just before daybreak.

I liked everything I was learning about Buddhism, with only one reservation: I was disturbed by the Buddhist attitude to the most central question of all: God. The Zen masters had spared no effort in order to have the same experience as the Buddha that fateful December dawn over 2,500 years ago. For the Buddha, that one experience had solved all the knotty problems of life: why we are born, suffer, grow old, and die. No wonder so many followers since his day have done everything they could to have the same experience, to turn themselves into buddhas, to achieve buddhahood. My one Zen retreat seemed ablaze with confirmation of everything I held dear in Christianity. But was that just the residue of centuries of conditioning and years of indoctrination in the Christian version of the truth. The question continued to nag: God or no-God?

As I was beginning to discover, the monk of whom I was so deeply suspicious on that first *sesshin* had come from Japan with impeccable credentials. His name was Sochu Suzuki Roshi, a Zen master of the strict Rinzai sect. Apparently, there were only about eighty such masters in the world. And he could name the lineage of spiritual masters who had passed the living teachings straight down through the centuries—from the Buddha in India to Master Rinzai in China, and then to Master Eisai, the key figure in bringing the distinctive Rinzai teaching to Japan, to his own teacher, to himself.

The practice of Zen sitting passed from spiritual master to novice, who in his turn became a master, and the lineage of transmission was unbroken. Hakuin, a master in the eighteenth century, was initiated by his teacher who advised him to concentrate on finding just two spiritual sons and training them until they reached Hakuin's own level of spiritual attainment. In Hakuin's time, Rinzai Zen was in decline and in danger of suffering an eclipse. But Hakuin was responsible for a great revival. It was he who invented the *koan* about the sound of one hand clapping. He was brilliant and imaginative and he wrote vividly—he describes himself sitting through the night in the graveyard where the wolves came and licked his nose.

Aside from his home temple, Hakuin only founded one training monastery—Ryutakuji (Dragon Pond Monastery)—which was where my teacher, Sochu Roshi, had come from. Sochu Roshi was soon made abbot of that very monastery. The abbot before him, Soen Nakagawa Roshi, was one of the Zen masters who could speak English and so had acquired a great reputation in America and other Western countries. Numerous Western followers had stayed at Soen Roshi's monastery to practice, including Paul Reps, Peter Matthiessen, and Robert Aitken.

Soen Roshi is known for having given a talk on the *koan* "Buddha nature is a shit-stick." It must be a bit like saying, "Stop worrying about whether Christ's nature was human or divine; it is really much closer to a piece of toilet paper than either." The talk was given in New York, and one of the founders of Xerox was present and was so impressed that he donated a fraction of the profits from Xerox to the Zen foundation in New York.

The Buddhist Society in London had originally invited Soen Roshi, but he could not spare the time. Sochu, his head monk at the time, suggested that he should go instead. Soen Roshi pointed out that Sochu did not speak a word of English. Sochu retorted that he would teach them with direct body language, no words. And that was how he first came to London to hold a Zen retreat in Eccleston Square.

Sochu Roshi returned the following year and spent more than six months in London founding the London Zen Society; that was in 1970. But shortly after that he succeeded Soen Roshi as abbot of the monastery, so he was too busy to be able to get away to London again for some time. Instead, he had asked Kyudo Roshi to visit the London Zen Society on his behalf. He and Kyudo had been close companions, spiritual brothers, throughout their arduous training in the monastery and after. Then Kyudo founded a Zen society in Jerusalem, where he was living when he was declared a Zen master by Soen Roshi. So Sochu Roshi (that is, Zen Master Sochu) and Kyudo Roshi were Soen Roshi's spiritual successors in a direct line of transmission that goes back to Shakyamuni Buddha.

If I had been born in Japan as a Buddhist, I would have been more than delighted to have become deeply involved with such men. But I was a Christian and profoundly attached to Christianity. Although I only realized it much later, this was typical of the tricks of the ego—to play off one good thing against another in order to avoid new challenges and new exertions, always preferring to remain stuck in the status quo.

Early in 1975, the very beginning of the Year of the Rabbit in the Eastern zodiac, Sochu Roshi had made time to visit London again. He held the Zen retreat that I attended—a *sesshin* that had lasted a full seven days, as in the monastery. At the end of it he had given me a picture he had painted of two white bunnies with pink ears. The bunnies were so soft and sweet—so very unlike that fierce retreat. Even before he left, he warned that the ordinary ego-mind would take over again. Sure enough, my ordinary ego-mind soon reasserted itself, quickly smothering the new outlook, the wonderful vista glimpsed on the retreat and for a little while after. It reminded me vaguely of something the first Christians had said about the old Adam and the new Adam. Old prejudices resurfaced, and my old outlook was creeping back.

In the year that followed, I certainly had misgivings. I was apprehensive about joining that little clique of Buddhists in London, and perhaps developing a ghetto mentality, in my own home town. For example, I feared my teachers might insist that I become vegetarian if I wanted to continue. Most of the other people who practiced Zen were vegetarian. Terence had given up meat and alcohol as well when he had first started practicing. It wasn't the meat I minded about so much; it was the bother, especially for my wife and my friends—and for me, if the bother caused me to lose them.

I was also afraid that I might lose my Christian faith, which was quite dear to me. I felt torn, and decided that what I really needed was a good Christian retreat, which would put me right. I have always loved the Christian monks, and it was through them that I recognized the value of the monks' life and could see that Sochu Roshi was a true monk. My experience with Christian monks made me feel at ease with the Buddhist monks from the start. I decided to go to Parkminster Monastery, where I'd been taken as a child, and had felt something of the presence of the Divine. I hoped to recapture my old love and so be able to give up the apparently conflicting new love for Zen that was growing in me.

I suppose that I was vaguely hoping that the example of the monks at Parkminster (who were the only ones in England of the strict Carthusian order, and lived almost like hermits) would extinguish my feelings about Zen. As it happened it did not work out like that. None of these monks were allowed even to visit other monasteries of their own order—not even the abbot. Occasionally, laymen would join them and participate in their monastic life. Male laymen, that is. When I visited, apparently a young man had just recently passed through after a long stay in a Japanese Zen monastery. The novice master of the abbey said he had never seen a person so transformed, so pure, so truly radiant. That was Father Bernard. I am told he is now the abbot there. He was afraid that his monastery had lost something of the former splendor of the order, in the course of all the persecutions and moves in recent centuries. He strongly advised me to keep with Zen. I shall always remain grateful to him and to that young man who happened to visit Parkminster and make such an impression on Father Bernard.

Sochu Roshi himself had told me that I had taken all he had to offer. I had done all I needed to do. And I half believed him. The fruit of that one Zen retreat would go on growing and maturing all my life. I was sure I would still remember it on my deathbed and be glad I had done that much at least. Surely a Buddhist monk would not have lied to me. But what he said was obviously untrue. You can usually recognize somebody who is further along the path you have chosen for yourself; inevitably they are the ones who have something special to offer you. "Do not be deceived by anybody," said an inner voice. "No, Master," Zuigan had said to himself. Perhaps that was why Sochu Roshi had told the story—before he lied to me. Deep inside myself, I knew that I had at last uncovered the entrance to the straight and narrow path that had eluded me for so long; I had found the long-lost entrance. But he was much further along the path. My mind's eye could see that clearly enough. He had started so much younger and worked at it so much harder than I could that the chances of catching up with him were slim. But at least I must set out, I thought.

Finally the year of waiting and dithering was over. Sochu Roshi took the cheap but uncomfortable Aeroflot flight from Japan via Moscow.

"Just do it" was one of his phrases that came back to me and rang through my head. Just go. Various problems cropped up, and I cut it fine to get there in time for his first sitting in the London flat. I was afraid I might be late, so I slid the door open very cautiously, listening for some sound that would indicate whether they had started. There was a reassuring shuffling noise. I quickly slipped my shoes off and turned. He stood in front of me with his arms stretched wide. His eyes were dancing with delight. My eyes met his and danced with them for a moment before we embraced. Then he was gone, back into the room where he'd been sitting—perhaps waiting for me anxiously, I don't know. There were plenty of cushions for me on the one spare mat.

The clappers and bells sounded, and we sat facing the wall. I really wasn't very good at it. A bit better than last year perhaps. But I should have done more in the meanwhile. It was not easy.

In the days that followed I nearly lost my nerve again about going on another Zen retreat—another seven days, but this time to be held in a *basement* on Randolph Avenue! I nearly did not go, partly because of Hélène, though I may have exaggerated her distrust of what I was doing, for when the retreat was over I mentioned to her that I had wavered at the last minute. Then she told me that she would have taken me and my bags and dumped us at the door and waved goodbye. She said it in that slightly different voice of hers that she reserved only for the times when she really meant what she says. It helped me a lot to know that she was really behind this, although she missed me and had to put up with a certain amount of aggravation and apprehension on account it. At least it meant I wasn't going to be required to choose between Zen and marriage. I couldn't help noticing that not many members of the London Zen Society were married. Was that connected with the fact that the teachers were monks? Was it Zen or marriage?

Was it Buddhism or Christianity?

I did not want to be disloyal to my age-old Christian commitment, but there it was. It could not be helped. This new love was overwhelmingly important—shatteringly important—to me. It seemed at the time that I had gotten more out of one week of Zen than I had gotten out of twenty-five years of Christianity. I dutifully kept up with my Christian practice, and because I was being fulfilled by other pursuits, it was not difficult to appear happy with it. I kept seeing new things in it that I had not noticed before and began to take a fresh delight in the Mass. But my heart was really elsewhere.

In my innocence, I half expected my second Zen retreat to start where the first one had left off. Whereas in fact it started just where the other one had started—with a lot of hard effort, sweat, and pain. The only difference was that I had some idea of what to expect—I knew there would be a turning point. I just had to hang on. Each time I went for the private interview during the first three days, Sochu Roshi just looked at me for a moment, assessing the situation in an impersonal way, and said, "Continue, continue." After the required three days of purgatory, I was sitting quietly elated when Sochu Roshi got up and moved stealthily around the room. Even in that silence he hardly made a sound. I wasn't quite sure if he was directly behind me or not. In any case it didn't matter as I was sitting perfectly well—if he was there he could only approve. Then *whack!* Out of the blue, his stick came crashing onto my shoulder. I was within a hair's breadth of losing my ear! What on earth had I been doing wrong? Usually when he was moving around, he never hit anyone unless they asked for it by putting their hands together and bowing. Or occasionally he would go around hitting everybody lightly when the whole room was in danger of dozing off. The blood had rushed to my face. Aggrieved, I braced myself and renewed my efforts. When I went for my private interview, he asked through his interpreter (a different Japanese layman than the year before) what I had felt when he hit me. He explained that I wasn't doing anything wrong but that a hit on the shoulder sometimes can help your mind's eye to open. However, he realized his mistake in my case and said he wouldn't do it again.

The next day he did it again—and it was as if my body had not been there at all. Though the noise was impressive, I could hardly feel the blow. But my body gradually returned to me, though as if made of glass at first, then of flesh—a truly magnificent affair made of flesh and blood. I am not especially squeamish, but I am just not very interested in the physical side of life as a rule. It was as if I had been missing the extraordinary intricacy of my own body. In its prime or past its prime, it did not make any difference—my body was truly a wonder.

In his talk the next day he said, "No inside, no outside." It brought to mind a tangled web of old ideas: subjective and objective experience, idealists and rationalists, nominalists and realists in the Middle Ages, Platonic ideas (where were they, anyway?), and Ockham's razor.

Later, during the last sitting before supper, Michael had gone out to prepare the meal. The sound of the wooden spoon knocking against the bowl in his hands went right through me. Then an airplane droned overhead—nothing between me and it, no barrier. Nothing to divide me from the world all around me. We were in vibrant contact with reality all the time. At my private interview with Sochu Roshi I said, "No inside, no outside." He was sure to understand since they were his own words, and they described the experience so precisely. But he wanted to know what I meant. I was trying to remember what had seemed so different and so special earlier. Then I thought, "But it's all around me all the time." And I looked around me and saw the bed, and it reminded me of Jesus saying that looking lustfully at someone is the same as adultery—in the mind or on the bed, the same. He smiled and rang the bell. But as I got up I realized it's so much simpler than that. All the people doing their Zen sitting beyond the wall, are they inside my head or outside? Sounds seep in through walls, but the mind has already seeped out over everything. It is already there dissolved in the universe, throughout the fabric of the universe. After that experience I noticed a new harmony growing, especially between me and other people as if they were really a part of me, or I of them.

In his next talk Sochu Roshi said, "Not just nice things. Not just pretty things. Everything good." And that evening, I stroked a pretty, long-haired, fluffy cat in the garden. Underneath its pretty fur it was a mass of lumps. I shuddered, but then, remembering today's talk, I felt the reaction of revulsion evaporate in a way that was new to me.

After the retreat was over, Sochu Roshi came to dinner with us. Hélène and he got on marvelously. It was rather similar to the way you don't notice the subtitles if the film is good enough—they conversed the whole evening, looking at pictures, demonstrating recipes, hardly aware of his limited English vocabulary.

Before he left England, Sochu Roshi organized a demonstration of painting and a sale of his calligraphy. For the demonstration, he dipped a twisted-up roll of paper towels into the black ink and with great energy inscribed a huge bold calligraphy on wall paper, which he liked because it was cheap, but also because of its texture. Then he did finer calligraphy next to it with a brush that had belonged to Master Hakuin over 200 years ago. He also did some Zen-style ink paintings. With the help of his Japanese-English dictionary, he had given the paintings titles. I especially liked his picture of three turnips, two big and one small, which he called *Eternal Vegetable*. He raised a good bit of money that weekend and donated it all to the Zen Society. He wanted us to find a house to use as a practice center.

When he left, I missed him.

Before Christmas, one of the members had found a house that was half the price of any on the market at the time, but in a terrible state of disrepair. From Japan, Sochu Roshi raised money for the mortgage through one of his supporters. He sent us all a calligraphy of a snake, as it was soon to be the Year of the Snake in the Eastern zodiac. Beneath the snake was written, "London *Zendo*: baby born. Happy New Year." And like a baby, the little house on Belmont Street needed a lot of attention. Dumpsters came empty and left filled with rubble and rubbish. By the time Sochu Roshi came again, the house was ready for sitting and a Zen retreat, but we had not done much to the top floor, which was going to be the monk's quarters. So Sochu Roshi again stayed with Hélène and me.

He took over the basement. In the daytime he sometimes popped up with a couple of little bottles of *saké*. After that, we occasionally went out searching dumpsters for things that would be useful in the new *zendo*, or "Zen training hall." We found a table, which he cut down and made into a makeshift altar, and other "dustbin treasures" as he called them. He built a fence around the front garden of the *zendo* out of wood collected from the trash. In the evening we often took him out to visit friends for dinner, or asked them over to visit.

One evening we went to Langham's Place, a local restaurant. As he entered, the whole roomful of sophisticated diners glanced up at him simultaneously, and for a short time the room was quite silent. Then the hubbub began again. He liked drinking, which made me wonder if we would get anything to drink in heaven? "Wisdom," he said firmly, holding up his glass. One exceptionally cold morning he even offered me a hot whiskey at 5:30 A.M. before we set off for the *zendo*. But every other morning it was strong green tea that was ready for me when I came down to drive him to the early morning sitting.

Before the Zen retreat started, Sochu Roshi warned me, "Perhaps no big fish waiting this *sesshin*." It was a good image. Four week-long *sesshin*s, and each time it had been as if I had caught a big salmon. But if there are no fish, then that's that. Nothing can be done. "It doesn't matter," I said. "Now we have the new *zendo*. That's more important." "Do you mean that?" he asked, so seriously that I had to think about it. I considered how the *zendo* would be there for a grandchild of mine, to practice Zen—and catch a fish. And the many people who might perfect their Zen practice there in the meanwhile. "Of course it's more important," I said.

He had sent a young, but fully trained, monk to stay at the *zendo*, and now, with a monk in attendance, Sochu seemed more like an abbot. When the younger monk (called Ichiyo) arrived the year before, I had spent quite a while teaching him English, and as a result I had learned more about Zen in Japan. In the past it had been quite customary for intellectually oriented Zen masters, like Soen Roshi, to have non-intellectually-oriented successors like Sochu Roshi, who in turn would find an intellectually oriented successor. This system had ensured that Zen attainment was never confused with intellectual attainment. It was not a question of talking about it.

Now, in Japan the old traditions were being eroded and university men were taking over the high positions and were becoming commentators—even though Dogen, eight hundred years before, had said, "Don't become a commentator. Spread your mat. Put your cushion on it, and do what the masters of old did. Sit, and become like them."

Each afternoon on retreat, Sochu Roshi gave a talk, with the young monk helping his "abbot" with the translation as best he could. One afternoon he said the whole of Zen could be summed up in one word. I asked what that word was. He just held up his thumb, which seemed to blaze before my eyes, and that said it all. I don't know if it was the thumb so much as the "no-word"—not even one short word—but I was satisfied with the answer.

One afternoon he talked about Case 14 in the *Mumonkan*, a classic Zen text containing forty-eight *koans*, commonly used in Rinzai Zen. In this *koan*, the monks in the west wing of the monastery were squabbling with the monks in the east wing about who owned a particular cat. The Zen master held up the cat and threatened to cut it in half, unless one monk could give him a convincing demonstration of why he should spare the cat's life. No one could, so he cut the cat in half. One of the monks was out at the time, but when he got back he was asked by his Zen master what answer he would have given. He took off his shoes put them on his head and walked out. "If only you had been there you could have saved the cat," the

Zen master said. That was in China, in the ninth century. And here was Sochu Roshi talking about it excitedly in London more than a thousand years later. "Upside-down people," he kept saying. "People all upside-down." Although I still felt sorry for the cat, it seemed a small price to pay to heal the rifts in monastic society from that day to this. If, by the simple act of holding me up and cutting me in half, Sochu Roshi could heal all the rifts in human society for the next thousand years, then surely it would be churlish not to oblige. But best of all was that monk's solution: as the master had commented, it really might have saved the situation without any slaughter or sacrifice at all.

As retreat continued, I began to feel much more supple. The next morning in the long sit before lunch, I managed the half-lotus position. For a while I was straining, but after an extra-long and fine outgoing breath, with a mind quite free of everything, suddenly it was as if my back fell back into its proper place. And so did everything else around me, like a foot fitting neatly into a shoe instead of being worn uncomfortably on the head as before.

Outside the wind was rising, roaring. It was again the time of the mad March gales. But despite the roaring winds there was a calm clarity of mind, and not just my own. In particular, the koans that had seemed so remote, riddles from the far side of the world and more than a thousand years ago, suddenly seemed custom-made for me—now, here in London.

Another koan tells of the young man waiting outside the gates of the monastery, begging for admission. He wanted to become a monk. After days of waiting in the snow, at last the abbot came and opened the gates wide, only to slam them on the young man's knee as he tried to enter. With a broken knee he fell back in the snow— enlightened. There was no longer any need to enter a monastery, Buddhist or Christian. Even Paradise itself might not be on the far side of the wall, beyond the gates. It was a psychological barrier that had to be torn down—and it could be torn down with Zen practice. Gates *then*, matched gates *now*, as if there were a mingling of minds that spanned thousands of miles and many centuries. Or just one mind.

It was not essentially different from what I had already experienced on that very first *sesshin*: pure mind dissolved in everything—and everything dissolved in pure mind. But it was clearer and more stable. Like a confirmation of the first experience. And by coincidence, outside was the sound of rushing wind. A bit later, as I stepped out of the *zendo*, I was met by a wind that whirled down and crashed at my feet, as if to corroborate that this was some form of spiritual confirmation. Back inside the *zendo* the Japanese screens that Sochu Roshi had made for the windows had been thrown from their hooks by the wind.

That evening as Sochu Roshi went off to bed, he whispered, "Have a good dream." And that night I dreamed that I was standing in the open air somewhere in the Near East, wearing a stole woven from silk, cotton, and wool. Silk from the Far East—I thought later—cotton from the Americas, and wool from the Mediterranean. It was as if the stole were the mark of some spiritual priesthood that would bring together three different strands of religion.

At the end of the retreat, Sochu Roshi handed me a work of calligraphy without much ceremony. In his private room, in front of a witness (a young Japanese man I only saw that once), he showed me a piece of calligraphy he had done. "Wisdom," he said, stuffing it into a very crumpled, brown paper bag. "Your new name: *Wisdom*." Wisdom was one of the seven gifts of the Holy Ghost that you were supposed to receive at the confirmation ceremony, and the one I had always liked best. (Later I learned the whole text read: "To Whole-Wisdom Layman. Enlightenment continue. *Mu* is the only way. Dated and signed: from Mind-Mirror, Sochu.")

I bowed. And as I came up my eyes were caught in the blazing dance of his eyes—more like the dance of lightning than fireworks, but in a way more dazzling than either. For a while our eyes danced together. It was hard to break from his gaze.

After the retreat was over Sochu Roshi came to my house for dinner. He was a delightful guest as usual, quite at home with us ever since he had stayed in the house that first time. But he asked to bring an American with him who had been staying in his monastery in Japan and now was studying in London. The American had shaved his head, yet had a huge beard that looked odd, as if his hair had slipped down under his chin and was standing on end. We all had quite a lot to drink. At one point the American put a glass on his shaven head and twirled it around with a meaningful grin on his face. My daughter assumed he was a bit daft and hoped that wasn't what happened to you if you did too much Zen. I hoped not, too. The image of me with shaven head—but wearing my sandals on top of it as I walked down Bond Street— flitted through my mind. I later mentioned it to Sochu Roshi, who asked me to tell the man the effect he had had, but I never did.

Before he left, Sochu Roshi asked me to buy a book for him. "After experience, books okay," he told me. It was a commentary on the *Mumonkan* by a Zen master named Shibayama. I got a copy for myself at the same time, and, with its help, got an increasingly profound respect for Zen *koans*. I also picked up a copy of Shunryu Suzuki's *Zen Mind, Beginner's Mind*. Slowly, with experience alternating with reading, I came to appreciate what a fine tool the *koans* were for distinguishing the subtle layers of spiritual truth, and for communicating this from generation to generation.

I presumed that Sochu Roshi wanted the book to give as a present to an English or American follower in Japan. When I took it up to him, the young monk Ichiyo was also there. I took advantage of the moment to ask about writing about Zen. They talked together in Japanese about it, then Ichiyo said that Sochu Roshi didn't want to read what I wrote. But was it all right to write about Zen at all, I asked, and if so, were certain things to be left out?

"Experience first, very important. Then writing okay." Through Ichiyo, he told me that too many books on Zen were written without any real experience, that I should write a simple direct book. I was his only writer, he said.

After Sochu Roshi had gone back to Japan, Ichiyo told me that I had given him a big present. I assumed his English was failing him again—what he really meant was Sochu Roshi had given me a big present. But no, Ichiyo was adamant that it was I who had given the present, so I left it at that, at the time not really understanding how it could be so.

In December of that year, the Year of the Snake, 1977, Ichiyo held a five-day *sesshin* ending at dawn on December 8th to celebrate the Buddha's enlightenment. The year before we had tried to do the same thing but nobody signed up to come, so Ichiyo and I had spent just one night in vigil. It had been pretty ghastly, like a long train journey sitting up through the night, being jolted awake occasionally.

This year, though, quite a few people came, and we all sat up through the last night. With a lot of cold splashes and walking around the block that cold night, I managed a bit better than I had the year before. Ichiyo sat bolt upright, and I did not see him budge once, though he may have done so while I was out. When the bell rang for the end of the sitting, it was about 5 A.M. and not yet dawn.

We all went out and there was a full moon with what looked like a silver pathway leading from the earth up to it. A moment later the trail of an airplane appeared above the moon, and the illusion was shattered. Ichiyo seemed amused that I was so impressed by this— the momentary illusion of a pathway to the heavens. It was the timing that impressed me.

I commented on how well he had sat compared with last year when we were both so thankful when it was over. He said the night-sitting had been for him the only good sitting of the whole *sesshin* because he didn't have to worry about the timing and the bells. (The sitting at night was informal, which meant there were no bells dividing the time into periods, and so you just shifted position when you need to do so.)

That morning it seemed as if the baby London *zendo*, born three years before, was beginning to be able to take a few steps on its own. It would need to—because Ichiyo was going back to Japan very soon.

3 INFINITE STEPS

"Life is a Marathon"

Ichiyo's father, also a Zen priest, used to race against Sochu Roshi when they were both boys at school. They were both sprinters, and so was I. Sprinting comes with a certain kind of mentality: you have enormous energy for the quick burst, but keeping things up steadily after that is another matter.

In the autumn after my first *sesshin*, Kyudo Roshi had visited London from Jerusalem. I took one look at him and left. I had some vague idea that you were only meant to have one Zen teacher, and stick with him. Once you had found the right teacher for yourself, you should not swap (which is something one is apt to do just when the training gets hard—a time when it is most important to be able to get help from a teacher with whom one has an established relationship). But I was also put off by something Kyudo Roshi said after the sitting. Someone in the room asked about prayer. He said that you could always try praying for something if you liked; you might get it and you might not, and he chuckled at the idea. It was ironic that it was *that* statement, of all things, that put me off. It made me think Kyudo Roshi might be one of those atheistic Zen masters who didn't mind whether there was a God or not. With my enthusiasm for Zen, I feared he might slowly corrode my trust that God hears my prayers. The idea of a Godless universe, with such powerful yet mindless forces at work, quite simply appalled me.

Kyudo Roshi came again a couple of times but I still stayed away. At one point, Sochu Roshi asked me if I liked Kyudo Roshi's *teishos*. "Good English speaking. Good *teisho*," he told me. I told him that I had never been on *sesshin* with him, so I had never heard him talk and didn't know if he was any good. Sochu Roshi seemed to realize the problem immediately, that it was partly out of loyalty to him that I had not gone. "Kyudo Roshi—me—same." He rubbed his two forefingers together. "Same—*Dharma* brothers." (That is, they were true spiritual brothers and themselves had had the same teacher.)

So the next time Kyudo Roshi came, I went for a second look at him, and he glanced at me too, after the sitting. Then he said to the room at large, "Life is not a sprint. Life is a marathon." He spelled it out in case we did not understand his pronunciation. I understood quite well. I had never even been able to manage the half-mile, let alone the cross-country. Life was indeed a marathon, not a mere bagatelle of twenty miles but twenty years, and then another twenty after that, and even then it was by no means over. And the going was heavy just then—my life was in a mess. "You must manage your life. You must manage your Zen. It's the same." He made gestures as if he were a TV set and turned the knobs; you had to have control otherwise you'd get a blurred fuzzy picture— a blurred, fuzzy life.

I signed up for his *sesshin* on the way out.

But it was the following year that something happened that left quite an impression on me. In the autumn of 1979, Kyudo Roshi visited London. I had gotten to know him a bit better by then, and when my turn came for my private interview with him, he asked me how I was. I had understood that these private interviews with a Zen master were strictly for talking about matters to do with Zen—how your sitting was going, and especially any interesting

Zen experiences you had while sitting. Kyudo Roshi had expressly asked us not to tell him how painful our knees were. He knew that already and had heard quite enough about it. So I started talking about my sitting, avoiding any mention of the knees. But he cut me short and said, "Your Zen is okay. But it is your writing you are worried about, isn't it?"

How right he was.

Three years spent at graduate school had not helped my career. Before I started Zen, I had tried to become a deacon in the Catholic Church. After recommending that I spend three years studying theology, and after spending another year to get a teaching qualification, the cardinal decided against making me a deacon. All that had set my writing back. On top of that, while still in school, I had started researching a book that had taken two more years to complete, but I could not find a publisher for it. Reluctantly I had put it aside and had been working for the past two years on a *Dictionary of Symbols*. But a new editor had taken over my work at Allen and Unwin (who had published my *Dictionary for Dreamers* seven years earlier). And he was not interested in the project on symbols. Certainly I was worried.

Kyudo Roshi said he would pray about it—but he didn't know if it would do any good. Sometimes his prayers got answered and sometimes they didn't. He chuckled.

I had also had a lot of fun devising a board game based on dreams: The Dream Game. It occurred to me a few weeks later that Granada, who'd published my dream book in paperback, might have a games division. They had all sorts of other things like television networks and motorway cafés, why not a games division? But they didn't have one. I had dealt with a string of editors there and knew nothing about the new editor who answered when I called about the game. Out of politeness this new editor inquired, apart from the game, what else was I working on at present? It so happened that he had been trying to buy a well-known *Dictionary of Symbols* by Cirlot for his paperback list, and his request for it had just been refused—he had the refusal letter on his desk. We met, and before the end of the year I had a contract and a large advance. If it wasn't the result of Kyudo's prayers, then it was a coincidence of a kind that was nonetheless so advantageous to me that I considered Kyudo Roshi to have been my spiritual agent in the affair. I gave him the percentage that would have gone to a more usual type of agent.

At the end of a long hard *sesshin* Kyudo Roshi once said, "Don't go away thinking now you understand Zen. You don't know anything about Zen. You are just beginners. Zen is very old, very deep. There is no end to Zen wisdom." He went on to mention the different collections of *koans* that were the beginning and basis of training for a Rinzai Zen monk. Apart from the *Gateless Gate* there were another hundred *koans* in the *Blue Cliff Record* and also another thirty-six *koans* in Master Rinzai's important collection, all displaying the hundreds of different aspects of perfecting and refining the spiritual wisdom of Zen.

A few days after that, I asked Kyudo Roshi if the Zen tradition had anything to say about the number of steps to heaven. At the time I was working on the symbolism of the various ladders to heaven with sometimes seven and sometimes eight steps and wondered if there was some equivalent in Buddhism.

"Infinite steps," he said sharply. "You are not there yet." In my imagination I could see them dwindling to infinity, like the old illustrations of Jacob's dream-ladder between heaven and earth, and it made me smile. He was watching me out of the corner of his eye.

More and more quickly, with less struggle and pain, the *sesshins* carried me down to a life that flowed through me—the very life that transformed bread and wine into body and blood for a while, until the body and blood dissolved back into earth and river. I enjoyed the Christian Mass most especially after a *sesshin*, when the readings often seemed so appropriate, and the ritual seemed especially meaningful. The transformation of bread and wine into flesh and blood—which reflected the ordinary transformations of nature and pointed to the living reality behind the ephemeral transformations of matter—evoked the bedrock of reality that must first be experienced from within, but could immediately be seen flowing throughout the universe and beyond.

The Christian Mass seemed more and more to be the celebration—or outward sign, as the penny catechism put it—of what had been accomplished for real on the Zen mat during *sesshin*: dying on the mat with Christ, disintegrating and dissolving in death like the water of humankind splashing and dissolving into the wine of God—first experienced, and then celebrated ritually, by the Christians of old through pure meditation.

The Science of the Soul

"You won't *need* to have sex any more," Kyudo Roshi said casually once, in the kitchen of the Zen Society building. "You can have it if you want to," he added quickly, perhaps because of something that passed across my face, "but you won't *need* to have it."

Of course I knew straight away what he was talking about: sexual compulsion and sexual sublimation, subjects that had been of burning interest to me in my teens, and were still of interest when Kyudo suggested in passing that the struggle was over.

Right from the very first *sesshin*, I had noticed two things: during the course of the *sesshin* I wasn't bothered by sex at all, and at the end of it I was extremely potent, without being especially randy or out of control about it. But that seemed natural enough to me. The work of sitting still, preventing the body from moving, was so incredibly exhausting, I presumed that it had just sapped my energy for anything else; and then by the time I got home presumably my body registered the fact that it was overdue.

It wasn't just me—I don't remember sex ever being a problem in the *zendo*. And on another occasion, Kyudo Roshi was telling us to do something special for our spouses when we got home, perhaps clean the bathroom. It is not proper *sesshin* if it makes no difference to your daily life. "Clean the bathroom," he said, "then your spouse will let you come to *sesshin* again." He went on to tell us about the wife of somebody in his New York group who said, "Take him on *sesshin* as often as you like, Roshi. Although I miss him dreadfully, when he comes back he makes love so beautifully—it's worth it." Roshi chuckled. "I'm a monk, so I don't know about that. But anyway, do something."

I was reminded again of a night, a year or two after I'd started practicing Zen, when I woke up extremely randy, burning and itching all over. Hélène was sound asleep and it seemed mean to wake her, so I went up and sat on the thick comfortable mat and cushions she had helped me make. The sensation might be compared to a wonderful midnight swim in the sea, naked alone in the moonlight. Somebody who has never sat *zazen* would not be able to imagine the pure joy that can come of it. And what I had presumed would be adverse conditions were positively helpful. I went back to bed completely refreshed, with a feeling of innocence that reminded me of a romanticized version of a time before puberty.

I got an inkling that I was very close to the place of sexual sublimation, that is to say, being able to transform the sexual drive into something else—and it did not require standing in freezing ponds with the ice forming around me—just pure contemplative prayer, just *zazen*. I became increasingly aware and sad that the rules for celibacy for Christian monks and clergy had outlasted the methods for achieving that state with honor. As Kyudo Roshi said once, a strong sexual drive is a help when it comes to the hard effort of Zen attainment.

But sexual compulsion is only part of a much bigger picture of relationship between ego and non-ego, between the conscious and subconscious. According to Jungian psychology, ego and shadow are two sides of every human being, like Dr. Jekyll and Mr. Hyde. Sexual compulsions arise from that part of the subconscious called the shadow. But like the ego, the shadow is also circumscribed, of fixed extent, both human-sized and human-shaped. It is a life's work to integrate the two and become a whole human being, seamless, without any split or conflict in the personality.

Despite extensive reading in Jungian psychology, the exact steps by which this is accomplished have always remained somewhat obscure to me. The books skillfully skirt around the essential question: What do you *do* about it? My work and research have concentrated entirely on what is of value to the ordinary individual working on one's own psyche, unraveling the complexities of one's own soul. In the logical style of the twentieth century, a great deal has been accomplished in terms of laying bare the issues, analyzing the components, and examining the parts. But when it's all put together, how to cope with the dynamics of ordinary everyday living is left curiously vague. One is left with vague hints—a personal description by one writer isolating herself on a hillside so as to make contact with her own shadow, for instance. Of course it's a help to know about the psyche—you can't *do* anything about it if you don't first *know* about it.

Westerners have been incredibly naïve in this respect, imagining that it will look after itself. Looking inward was still commonly referred to as "morbid introspection" when I was beginning to read Jung—as I tried to discover what my imagination was telling me about the dynamics of my soul and the inner workings of my psyche. For those who have neither the urgent incentive (usually inner problems that are having a disastrous effect on everyday life), the time, nor the funds to enter an analysis, what should they do? What is the practice involved? Once fully convinced and committed to the ideal of living life for the sake of soul, how do you set about doing it? What, specifically, should you actually do?

One famous Jungian analyst advises that everything counts, from the first dream remembered in childhood to the last conversation on your deathbed. He suggests that there are many ways of soul-making, but whatever the end product, however distinctive and different, what is wonderful is the finely wrought soul. The loss of youth is compensated for by a special newfound graciousness in age. This is what I have always believed. And sometimes—not often—I have seen it with my own eyes.

Some patients in psychoanalysis, when healed and about to rejoin the other people in the human pen, have asked their Jungian analysts what they should do next. In several recorded cases they were advised to return to the religion of their childhood. And for good reason: throughout recorded history and no doubt long before, religion has been the context in which soulwork was carried out. Soulwork is not only individual, it is communal. It affects all of society. But not only that, the work of personal development inevitably contributes to the evolution of the human soul in the course of centuries. Individually and through culture, one's personal development affects subsequent generations drastically for better or worse.

When it comes to soulwork there is a very considerable overlap between the study of the soul, in the form of psychology, and spiritual training, or direct work on the soul, which could be considered a major constituent of all religion. Soulwork is of such vital importance to the human race that it needs to be perpetuated—whether the form remains religious or not.

The ego has many delusions and limitations. The ego of Western people is particularly identified with the intellect and with the senses. It would be difficult to convince us that we have a fuzzy view: to us the world looks pristine, and we have hardly a shadow of doubt that we have the whole picture clearly in sight. This picture is clear enough, but limited. From this particular ego base, the human psyche can feel very self-assured, precisely because its outlook is so limited and superficial. This particular ego mentality is reinforced by the majority, which shares a similar limited view. As a result, feeling and intuition have been woefully neglected, and they have erupted in an erratic and irrational form with quite disastrous consequences.

If it were only sexual compulsions that the ego could not control, perhaps there would not be so much cause for concern. As it is, I sometimes see the figure of the human maniac, the drunk in charge of the dangerous vehicle of the human psyche. His eyes are horizontal, his nose is vertical, and he's an egoist—like me. I know all about him.

This is why the transformation of the ego is so important both for psychology and religion. The final goal of Jungian psychology is the transformation of this very ego into the true self, which can be likened to the transformation of the acorn into the oak tree, or the egg into the bird of paradise. And it is in this work that meditation is extremely helpful—and may even be indispensable. In fact, Jung himself meditated.

The ordinary ego consciousness sees everything according its own preconceived ideas. Even the most broad-minded people, with the widest possible human view, perceive reality through the filter of ego, with its particular set of senses and bent of mind. But still, this remains our *perception* of reality, not reality as it is. Although you may never be able to know reality as it is in itself, you can most certainly allow for the fact that there is something beyond what you perceive and independent of the way you perceive it.

This direct apprehension sometimes comes in a flash. It is a realization that spreads through life on the surface and affects it dramatically. It is something that comes from beyond the depths of the individual soul, from the spirit, and it reflects something at work throughout the universe. It is most often experienced through meditation when the ego is annihilated. The individual erases his or her ordinary outlook, throws the plumb line into the deepest reaches of human life, and just keeps on letting out the line. In mediation, since you are cutting out thought and rooting out images, you eventually and almost inevitably reach a state without thought or image. But you are also emptied of *nothing*. You may pass through a stage of sinking into a black abyss, a negative emptiness, but this too is just an idea.

It is a powerful experience and corresponds, in my mind, to the indwelling Spirit of God, stripped of all images and preconceived ideas. Although the experience is totally empty, it is empty in the manner of the womb of nature. Anything could come out of it, and, as it happens it has. This very world has come out of it, and each of us with our particular set of senses to perceive it. This is the relative world. Everything only appears as it does because of a vibrant relationship with the senses, with the mind and the way it is made. But since both mind and world come from the same source, there is no need to apportion which contributes what. Reality becomes whole and seamless again—just it, reality as it is. Nor is it in any way separate from the empty womb: the teeming city and the empty womb both manifest the same reality.

The ego is an alien. It has alienated itself, and protects its position. Once cut off, it is embattled. It is also short-lived and therefore frightened, whereas the non-ego—everything that is not "you"—is eternal. When you are able to identify with larger reality, as opposed to the small-minded ego, your are no longer cut off, no longer short-lived. As St. John the Divine said: "To know God, that is eternal life."

I do not doubt that the distinction between the ego and non-ego could be deduced and analyzed by the intellect. But you cannot possibly deduce the full extent of the gulf between experiencing the world from within the narrow confines of the ego, and experiencing it, even for a short while, from the detached free viewpoint of non-ego. It comes out of the blue, quite unexpected—and exceeds all expectations.

The Zen masters I have met, Sochu Roshi and Kyudo Roshi, seem to live from this perspective consistently. Not that they don't have egos, but their particular egos are just part of the much wider perspective from which they live and relate to everybody and everything around them. It is typical that, although the people who turn up at the Zen Society come from such diverse cultures and backgrounds, these masters have so little difficulty relating to each of the great variety of individuals. Even the language barrier is dissolved. Sochu Roshi and Kyudo Roshi seem to me very pure and untramelled, in a very natural way. And *that* is what requires such extremes of effort. It seems to me that Shakyamuni Buddha and Jesus Christ, in their very Buddhahood and their Christhood most especially, were forerunners of this worldview arising from non-ego—a limitless and eternal view that they shared with their followers. And it gave them a particular relationship with the organized religion of their respective time and place. They saw through the religion into which they were born, to what religion had always been leading toward and pointing at: the essential nature of life, ordinary conscious life—which we each can get to know with clarity and intimacy. In the cases of Jesus Christ and Shakyamuni Buddha, what they revealed was a new universal Spirit of Truth, which left the old religions intact, but thrown into a new perspective.

In this process, the ordinary ego viewpoint becomes increasingly transparent, and, in the spiritual masters of humankind, eventually vanishes. In Christian terminology, this is the apotheosis of humanity, the truly human and the truly divine, combined in the same person—the person of an ordinary Christian receiving communion at Mass. The essence of the Divine life is infused into bread and then eaten; thus, a perfect and real moment in the cosmic process of the Divine life is turned into you and then turned into the universe, to make a suitable home for you and me. The home is real and so are we—real, ordinary, and everyday, but not banal.

Last Stop, First Step

The wooden clappers banged together. Tea was over, and the teapots were taken out for the last time. The brass bar struck the brass bell, and the last period of *zazen* began. Soon *sesshin* was over. This moment seemed to be the ultimate goal of all that had gone before, the final fruit of all past processes. But it is also a totally fresh start; it is equally the seed of all future life—the fruit and the seed simultaneously.

At the airport we bowed our goodbyes to Kyudo Roshi, who waved good-bye as he disappeared into the departure lounge.

I took the subway to Euston Station to catch a train to Stafford, expecting to arrive in time for Sunday lunch with Hélène. Maddeningly there was construction on the line. Instead, I had to take the Manchester Express and change at Stoke-on-Trent, far beyond Stafford. I was meant to be phoning Hélène around 1 P.M., or else arriving by taxi soon after, for Sunday lunch together. She would be anxious and cross. I buried myself in my book and was particularly struck by a section on the "I am" sayings of Jesus: "I am the living water and bread of life." It reminded me of my first taste of Zen, the sense of pure being—"*I am*"—with Sochu Roshi, nearly twenty years before.

I was deep in my thoughts, when the train drew to a standstill in the middle of nowhere. An unscheduled stop—more delays. I glanced out the window and read a battered and faded small sign on an old-fashioned lamppost that said "Rugeley." There could only be one Rugeley, surely, the nearest shopping town to my apartment. I grabbed my bag, leaped out onto the platform, and shut the door after me. I just had time to take in the length of that great Manchester Express: only two of its many carriages fitted opposite the platform; only one window was alongside the one small sign. Already the train was gathering speed, making up for lost time, no doubt. The lamppost looked as if it used to be lit by gas. The wooden footbridge was very rickety. It was just a few minutes before 1 P.M. when I called Hélène and asked her to pick me up, but at Rugeley Station, not Stafford, on the Uttoxeter Road out of Rugeley. I would be at the pub opposite the out-of-use station, I said, and would explain the whole thing.

I sat outside with a pint of beer. It was compelling to think that the universe was somehow conspiring to support me: the Manchester Express letting me off at Rugeley so I would not be late for my lunch date. Later it reminded me of a Zen arrow effortlessly hitting its mark—the mark, the arrow, and the man, all one. That long straight train, shot from London and arriving bang on target, a small circular target, dangling from an old lamppost, with "Rugeley" written across it. Although it was ridiculous, I could not help feeling that Kyudo Roshi had a hand in it, too. I hoped for him that he would get a bit of a rest when he got home to Japan. And more especially that among the new monks he would find some true followers, who would go the whole way—who would achieve buddhahood and be able to step into his shoes when he steps out of them.

He worked so hard, Kyudo Roshi—and Sochu Roshi before him—to bring a handful of Europeans to full realization. And it was uphill work. There were so few prepared to throw their full weight behind that wheel of effort, to struggle up to the crest of the hill. And they were the culmination of a long line of tradition going back 2,500 years and more. Suddenly that seemed to be what was truly remarkable: the Zen transmission was just such an express train, happening to make an unscheduled stop at Rugeley, within walking distance of my home in London. Just for me to get on or off as I chose—and to take what I liked from it.

In the long story of Zen, there are many who achieve enlightenment and then just delight in it—bowling around the back alleys of life, poets and wastrels enlightening one or two others if they get the chance. I suppose that's all right, too. If it wasn't for their delightful example, not many people would start on the arduous training necessary. But personally, as I sat sipping my beer in the sunshine at the pub opposite the station no longer in use, I could not help being more grateful to those who had worked so unstintingly to transmit the universal truth from one generation of spiritual followers to the next, until the opportunity to experience it finally reached me.

Our small, red car rounded the bend in the road. Hélène jumped out of the car and we embraced. It seemed as if millions of years culminated just there, just then—and they did, of course. I showed her the derelict station where the train had stopped, before we drove off up the hill, going home for lunch.

The Investigation

By the time I started looking for the traces of Christian meditation and piecing together the story, I already had a strong hunch there would be parallels with Zen.

It is true that when I first read the four Gospels—straight through on a single summer afternoon at school—it did not occur to me that Jesus Christ practiced and taught meditation. But on the other hand, how else could he have transformed his followers?

When I studied theology, I had been particularly interested in the Kingdom of Heaven, which was the central and most important part of Jesus Christ's teaching, yet no very satisfactory explanation of it was ever provided. Jesus Christ's followers seemed always to be asking about it, in rather the same way that people who practice Zen often ask about enlightenment.

From my experience at the Zen society, I could well understand how many of Jesus Christ's followers might have gotten the wrong end of the stick, and gone off with quite the wrong idea—especially since his teaching career was cut somewhat short.

Early in my investigations I turned to the Desert Fathers, early Christians renowned for their spiritual training. But, more importantly, they seemed to reflect the teaching of Jesus Christ, particularly with regard to the Kingdom of Heaven, and they were close to the first Christian communities, both geographically and in time. They believed in the relationship of spiritual master and novice and in a spiritual initiation that broke down the barrier to the Kingdom of Heaven. But there was, however, also a lot of seemingly outlandish and curious material in the various contemporary accounts of them that made my mind reel.

For example, one account told the story of a young monk who had it in his mind to go to the inner desert and see if there was any man living therein. He went on a journey of four days and four nights and found a certain cave. Having approached the cave he looked inside and saw a man sitting therein, and he knocked at the door, according to the custom of the monks, so that the person inside might come out and the monk might salute him, but the man in the cave never moved—for he was dead. The monk did not hesitate or draw back, but went in and laid his hand upon the dead man's shoulders, and the dead man crumbled into dust and became nothing at all.

Another account advised eating grass: "Eat grass, wear grass, sleep on grass, and your spirit will become like iron."

As I read about Anthony of the Desert on one of the late evenings at the British Museum reading room, I was reminded of what the Zen Master Dogen had said in the thirteenth century: "Look at Buddha, who sat for six years, and consider the fame of Bodhidharma, who faced the wall for nine years. This is what the old sages did; why not the people of these days?" Anthony of the Desert "dwelt in a place that was like unto a cleft in the rocks," and "he had his abode there for very many years." When, after many years, Anthony emerged from that place, "his appearance was like unto that of an angel of light," and the people marveled that his body "had not been weakened by all his confinement, and why it was that his understanding had not become feeble." His fame spread to Emperor Constantine in Rome, just as the fame of Bodhidharma reached the emperor of China. Anthony was said to be 105 years old when he died, with his face full of joy. It was said after his death, his face "resembled that of a man when he sees a friend whom it rejoiceth him to meet." But he arranged to be buried in a secret place, "because the Egyptians were in the habit of taking the dead bodies of righteous men, and of embalming them, and of placing them not in graves, but on biers in their houses, for they thought that by doing so, they were doing them honor."

A bell rang to indicate that the library would be closing shortly. I put the markers with my name on them in the books to reserve them and went to the counter with Anthony's words ringing in my head: "Permit no man take my body and carry it into Egypt, lest they embalm me and lay me up in their houses, for it was to avoid this that I have come here."

I stepped out under the huge colonnades of the museum. It was a misty evening in late autumn, and the starlings were massing on the trees and rooftops, getting ready for their annual migratory trip to Egypt. Something startled them, so they circled and chattered and settled again. The starlings were on their migratory way to modern Egypt, and I was on my way back from ancient Egypt—it was taking time to reach London in the twentieth century. I did not want to risk negotiating the steps until I had gotten my balance and my bearings. It took a moment to gather my wits about me.

But in that moment I noticed how widespread my wits were, and how deep—just naturally so. It was if I had been riding the spirals of DNA for thousands of years. At that moment I realized that it was life that lent the universe its own extent and depth. The starlings were lively enough, chattering in the trees and on the rooftops—but they did not know the distance to the Milky Way, or that there were stars in it that were bigger than the sun. And what did the sun know about its own sunspots or size? As for the trees, they are enormous and sinewy with life, but barely aware of the difference between night and day, as Blythe pointed out in his *Zen in English Literature*. And as for the stones, they would have no reality at all but for the living; no hardness or heaviness but for the abundance of life, of which we are the carriers. Suddenly I understood something I'd read in Jung about man being the second creator of the universe.

I took the steps like a wary old man, but I was soon striding the pavement and dodging the traffic of the city where I was born like a schoolboy. At other times I felt like a monk, just emerging from the monastery library after researching the sequel to the New Testament. Just one particular life among so many—the only one I had to cope with, so far as living it was concerned.

Just then I particularly appreciated the gift of having learned how to meditate from Sochu Roshi, and I appreciated the light that gift was throwing on the story of Christian meditation.

The most compelling reason for a Christian to start meditating would be that Christ himself practiced and taught meditation. But the sequel to the story of Christ was important too, and my aim in telling it will be much like that of John Cassian, a Christian monk in the fourth century, who states:

> I do not believe a new establishment in the West could find anything more reasonable or more perfect than are those customs observed in the monasteries throughout Egypt and Palestine, founded by holy and spiritually minded fathers since the rise of the apostolic preaching.

PART TWO

Christian Meditation in the Light of Zen

Why have you given up everything and come here?
We replied: "We did it for the Kingdom of Heaven."
Yes, but the immediate purpose of our profession
is purity of heart. Should it ever happen
that for a short time our heart turns aside from
the direct path, we must bring it back again at once,
guiding our lives with reference to our purpose,
as if it were a carpenter's rule.

John Cassian, Christian monk (ca. 360–440)

The Kingdom of Buddha is in this world
Within which enlightenment is to be sought.

Hui Neng, Sixth Zen Patriarch (638–713)

The first thing is that you should know the invisibility
of your mind, before you can become capable
of the knowledge of the invisible God.

Richard of St. Victor, Augustinian Monk (d. 1175)

4 THE STORY OF CHRISTIAN MEDITATION

The Background

For Zen, the essential starting point is Zen sitting (*zazen*). *Zazen* leads to the experience of pure mind (*samadhi*), into which breaks enlightenment as a sudden experience and as the gradual maturing of spiritual insight (*satori*). In the original practice and teaching of Jesus Christ, there would appear to be the equivalent or counterpart of each of these: Through pure, conptemplative prayer and meditation, a change of heart leads to purity of heart (heart being the depths of the mind) and to the realization of the Kingdom of Heaven. In the East, The Way of Heaven (*Tao*), and the Universal Law (*Dharma*) are not unrecognizably different from the Kingdom of Heaven and the Divine Reign in Christian terminology. Nor is the essential nature of the individual and the universe so very different from the Christian concept of the Spirit, also at work within the individual and throughout nature. There are further parallels between the Zen *koans*, which cannot be understood by the intellectual ego, and some of Jesus Christ's sayings and parables, which cannot be understood by those who have not been initiated into the mystery of the Kingdom. Similarly, the *koans* become accessible, and even simple, after Zen experience.

On the Christian side, what was hard to find were the particular instructions about how to meditate, the specific details about the ideal circumstances for a spiritual breakthrough. Having decided to put the Kingdom of Heaven first, what should one do next? The more I researched Christian methods of meditation, preserved intact century after century, the more they seemed like Zen methods.

In this chapter, I have arranged the quotations and extracts from the story of the Gospels and its immediate sequel—the story of Christian meditation, the texts from the Desert Fathers—and the instructions of the later Christian spiritual masters as follows:

1. Texts on the skills and craft of meditation (the process);
2. Texts on pure mind (the state achieved);
3. Texts on the Kingdom of Heaven (the result).

The Buddha Was a Christian Saint, but Was Christ a Buddhist Sage?

When it comes to forging a new link in the chain of spiritual transmission from master to master, it may become important to study in depth the already existing links between Buddhism and Christianity. However, we cannot do more than offer a preliminary sketch of the ground to be explored.

First, consider the infiltration of the edifying story of the Buddha into the Arab world, and from there into the whole of Christendom. There was a Christian feast in honor of him, churches dedicated to him, and ballads that sang the story of his life—including one in medieval English.

It is thought that this may have come about through the agency of the Manichaean Christians, who lived in the same communities as Buddhists on the great Silk Road from China to Rome. One researcher has suggested that it was these Christians who introduced the story to the Arabs, who corrupted one of Buddha's titles, "Bodhisattva" into "Josaphat" and called Buddha's ascetic teacher "Barlaam." Christian elements that are not in the oldest Arabic version have crept into later versions of the story.

Only in the nineteenth century did this scandal break. For a while, a few die-hard Christian scholars clung obstinately to the hypothesis of an altogether different Christian Indian saint. They wrote angry footnotes in their now obsolete histories, insisting that this saint was not to be confused with the Buddha as some were suggesting.

More recently, in his popular revision of Butler's book about lives of the saints, Donald Attwater has this entry:

> Barlaam and Josaphat. No Date. Feast Day 27 November. These "saints"...are the principal characters in a fictional narrative adapted from the Indian story of Siddhartha Buddha.

Indeed, even at the end of the nineteenth century, there were still people who refused to believe that a story alleged to be from the pen of that most glorious of Confessors, St. John of Damascus, could be about the Buddha. Baring-Gould delivers a telling blow to these holdouts, writing:

> The story of Barlaam and Josaphat is a Buddhist legend of the youth of Gotama Buddha.... The Brahmin hermit [his tutor] was made a Christian ascetic. St. John Damascene was no doubt himself thoroughly deceived in the matter. He lived amidst Mussulmans, and not Buddhists, and the Mohammedans probably mistook Indian Buddhists for Christians.... Baronius was probably unaware that he was introducing him [Buddha] into the Roman martyrology when he adopted his legend from St. John Damascene. The story of Barlaam and Josaphat found its way into the *Golden Legend* of Jacques de Voragine and into the *Gesta Romanorum*, and was translated into most European languages. There is even an Icelandic version of it.

This gives some indication of the ferment of ideas in the Middle East—a great crossroads of human culture and civilization—the meeting of three continents—Asia, Africa, and Europe—and the birthplace of Judaism, Christianity, and Islam. These are the three great Western branches of the tree of world religion. The three other major branches are those of the East—Hinduism, Buddhism, and Taoism. One researcher has even traced substantial links between Judaism and Hinduism. The present day dialogue between these faiths makes it increasingly desirable to investigate more closely the situation in the ancient Near East.

In the past, the tendency was to isolate the different strands of religion in the vague, but vehemently felt, hope of preserving some ill-defined purity of the particular belief or faith. But the considerable danger in this approach is increasingly to parochialize (and thereby trivialize) what was originally of far more universal significance. The thorough investigation of the origins of Christianity, however, has tended to show that elements from other traditions were present in it from the start. These elements are of a universal nature, perhaps contributing to Christianity's appeal.

Jesus Christ taught after Alexander the Great had forged ties with India—resulting in the first statues of Buddha being sculpted in a mainly Greek style. Later Buddhism spread rapidly when Emperor Ashoka sent Buddhist missionaries to the West as well as the East, missionaries that Mackenzie suggested may even have reached England. The presence of Indian *sannyasi* were noted in Egypt, and called by the Greeks the "naked wise men" (*gymnosophists*). These naked wise men were particularly prevalent near Alexandria, which was an important center for the pepper trade between India and Rome. Against this background of plain facts of empire and trade stands the far more elusive world of trade in ideas: the Pythagorean belief in reincarnation; the ideas of the Neo-Platonists and Origen, which may have stemmed from the precepts of the Buddha Shakyamuni (whose name was corrupted to Ammonius Sakkas). Against this background, scholar Roy Amore has made a preliminary survey of the parallels between the life and teaching of Shakyamuni Buddha and of Jesus Christ in *Two Masters, One Message*.

But so far, what is still lacking is a scholarly study of the wealth of material from the Dead Sea Scrolls, looking for loan words and parallels with earlier Buddhism from the sixth century B.C. In the late nineteenth century there was a lively scholarly debate about the possible influence of India in general and Buddhism in particular on the Essene communities, as indicated in the *Hastings Encyclopedia of Religion*. The question is, how can we explain the sudden appearance of monastic-style communities among the Jews? Monastic life is not a Jewish custom, nor even a Semitic phenomenon—and it was even condemned by Mohammed. But it is certainly an Indian—and especially a Buddhist—phenomenon. India was Buddhist in the centuries before Christ, when the Essene communities were founded.

If a link were to be established between the Jewish monastic community life and Buddhist monastic customs, this would then suggest a line of spiritual initiation and transmission linking the twin trunks of world religion, East and West.

In the meantime, without completely dismissing this background, it is enough to trace the one authentic and pure strand of Christian spiritual practice: that is to say, the practice of meditation, taught by master to novice, from Christ himself, almost up into the present time—but not quite.

If Jesus Christ is to be placed in this continuing line of spiritual practice, then one essential ingredient must be that he be instructed in the spiritual way of life, like the Buddha before him, who left his home to follow an older spiritual teacher. Of this we are told almost nothing—but then it is human nature to dismiss the hard effort that lies behind all human accomplishment and just look at the results as if they were bestowed as a boon to one rather than another. All one can say is that there was time for

Jesus Christ to undertake this individual responsibility, to be taught the spiritual way, so that in due course he could teach it. Between the time of his birth (after which he was taken to Egypt), and the moment he emerges as a mature teacher some thirty years later, we are told of only one incident, when the boy Jesus stayed behind in the city of Jerusalem. But in the light of a letter (to which we shall return) by Clement of Alexandria, which suggests that the Gospels, as we have them, were only the most superficial form of the true Christian teaching (which was kept a carefully guarded secret for those who had been initiated), it seems to me justifiable to look for a deeper significance to this one recorded incident in the first thirty years of Jesus Christ's life. The Gospels mention this incident:

> When his parents set out for home, the boy Jesus stayed behind in Jerusalem. They returned to Jerusalem and on the third day they found him. He was in the temple sitting among the teachers and putting questions to them as well as listening to what they said. Everyone who heard him was amazed at the understanding he showed in his replies.
>
> "Did you not know that I must be about my Father's business?" Jesus said to his parents.

I think the real significance of this scene is a meeting with his spiritual teachers at the age of twelve, which would be the age to start his spiritual training. The Qumran community was active in the temple of which they claimed to be the legitimate priests, and this community is a plausible background for the teaching of Jesus. After such an encounter, would a spiritual teacher in the making continue with his instruction? It is plausible that it was "under the direction" of his spiritual teachers that "Jesus increased in wisdom and stature, and in favor with God and man."

Yet the question remains: once Jesus had discovered spiritual teachers, and displayed his dazzling gift to them, is it likely that he would spend only three days doing the work of his true Father?

Did Jesus Christ Meditate?

The practice of *zazen* is a very precise discipline. When practicing, it is essential to follow the instructions very exactly. It is worth reading and trying out each particular detail of the method of *zazen* given in Sekida's book *Zen Training. Zazen* is a method of meditation not to be confused with any other, and the whole success of the enterprise depends on this. It is not for dabblers.

Some Zen masters don't like *zazen* being called "meditation." Kyudo Roshi contrasts *zazen* to "meditation," saying: "Meditation is nice and easy: a comfortable chair, a glass of wine, sit back and relax. Zen is not like that. No."

Nevertheless "meditation" is the usual translation of the Indian word *dhyana*, which is the original source of the Japanese word *Zen*. It derives from *dhyana yoga*, the yoga of meditation. And the word "meditation" is probably the best general-use word left to convey what a Zen monk does—namely *zazen*, which translates as "Zen sitting."

Similarly, in the Christian tradition, the word "prayer" was used for pure contemplative prayer, without any object in view, without any thought or image in mind. Zen masters recognize the similarity between their *zazen* and pure contemplation. But the word "contemplation" in common usage means something quite opposite to pure meditation—it is defined as gazing upon; expecting; intending.

Furthermore the word "prayer" is mostly used to refer to prayers of petition, begging the powers that be for bicycles and fine weather. Traditionally, this was the lowest form of prayer in the Christian hierarchy. Jesus Christ said of it, "God knows your wants before you ask Him, so there is no need to ask." And nobody would want to suggest that Jesus himself was capable only of prayers of petition. But this is precisely what is suggested by the word "prayer" to most Christians unfamiliar with the Christian contemplative tradition.

From the Desert Fathers after Christ, who traced their teaching directly back to him and the first Christian communities, we can learn something of the details of their pure meditation, and from that, deduce the way Christ himself would have prayed in the solitudes of Judea, often throughout the night.

For me the word "prayer" now seems inadequate, so in reading the Bible, I have substituted "meditation," which seems to me the best word to suggest what the Buddha taught, what a Tibetan yogi does, what a Zen monk does, what St. Anthony did when walled up in a cleft in a rock in the deserts of Egypt, and what Jesus Christ did in the wilderness.

It has not been emphasized sufficiently among Christians how much time Christ devoted to the practice of meditation and how often meditation is mentioned, even in the canonical Gospels. Such phrases as, "He spent the night in meditation directed to God," and "He often retired into the solitudes to meditate" are but two examples. The Gospels also say of Jesus:

> As he meditated the aspect of his face was changed and
> his clothing had the brilliance of a lightening flash.

Jesus Christ, Teacher of Meditation

When Martha was busy getting the meal ready and asked Jesus to make Mary help her, Jesus replied: "You are troubled about many things. But one thing is needful." According to the Desert Fathers and all later Christian tradition, the one thing needful for the Christian life, of which Christ was speaking, was pure contemplative prayer (meditation). Jesus Christ said:

Look to yourselves, lest at any time your faculties be
numbed by the cares of life.... Keep awake, meditating at
all times.

Jesus Christ often exhorts his followers to "watch," which is
sometimes directly linked with meditation, "watch and meditate."
Sochu Roshi used the word "watch" to describe right attention in
zazen. He would tell us to watch like a cat at a mousehole: If you are
too relaxed, you won't be ready to pounce; on the other hand, if you
strain too hard, you'll get exhausted and fall asleep, and go hungry
just the same. Jesus Christ offered a similar teaching:

Watch then, for you do not know when the master of the
house is coming back—in the evening, at midnight, at
cock's crow, or at dawn. What I say to you, I say to everyone: Watch.
   Watch therefore. You may be sure that if the owner of
the house had known at what hour of the night the bur-
glar was coming, he would have stayed awake.

To this day, many Zen monks persevere with their *zazen* night
and day, especially during the great December retreat (*robatsu
sesshin*), which culminates on December 8, celebrating the morning
of Buddha's enlightenment upon seeing the morning star. Anyone
familiar with an effective method of meditation will know that it
takes much time for the mind to settle and clear. The hard effort
involved is something like a determined banging at a door. Because
people were sitting in too relaxed a manner, Kyudo Roshi once took
a cushion and tapped against the wall with it: "A thousand years—
it'll never break through," he said.
   Another afternoon one of the teachers at the London Zen Society
took us out to Primrose Hill, and we did *zazen* there. The grass was
soft and inviting, and there was a cool breeze. He could have given

his afternoon talk there, but he didn't. It made me wonder about Jesus taking large crowds out into the wilderness, the very place where he went to meditate and fast, and was tempted to turn stones into bread. What did they do there? Four complete lives of Jesus could be read in an afternoon, so his sermons would scarcely be any longer than a Zen talk, an hour or two at the most. But on one occasion they were in the desert for three days. Nothing is explicitly said about meditating, yet it would not be untypical to record what was said, while omitting mention of the long hours of silent meditation, which are not especially riveting to read about.

> During these days there was once more a great concourse of people. As they had nothing to eat, he called his disciples to him and said: "I feel sorry for all these people who, for three days now, have attached themselves to me and have had nothing to eat. If I send them home starving, they will faint on their way—and some of them have come from far."
>
> His disciples answered: "Here in the wilderness, where could one find enough bread to satisfy these people?"
>
> He told the people to settle down on the ground.

There are variations of the same story and other similar occasions. In some accounts the people were arranged in groups and squares, which could have been just for the picnic—but what they did, the rest of the time, still invites thinking about.

The crowds flocked around their teacher, Jesus Christ. But they also flaked off fast, as is stated quite explicitly in the Gospels: "Many of Jesus's disciples fell away and no longer went about with him."

The excuses have a familiar ring for anyone who's ever practiced Zen for long. The same excuses then and now. Everybody wants to come on a Zen *sesshin*—if only they had the time. They fully realize what a wonderful opportunity it is to encounter a Zen master and hear his teachings—but unfortunately this time there is cousin being buried in Cumberland. Jesus Christ seems to have encountered something of the same difficulty.

> "The Kingdom of Heaven," [he said,] "is like a King who was celebrating his son's marriage. He sent out his servants: 'Tell the guests that I have prepared my wedding breakfast; my bulls and fatted cattle have been killed and all is ready.'
>
> "But they took no notice and went off, one to the farm he owned, another to his shop."
>
> [And on another occasion] one of Jesus' fellow guests said: "Happy the man who dines in the Kingdom of God."
>
> But Jesus said to him: "There was a man who was giving a big dinner party. He sent out his servant to remind the people that everything was ready. But they all with one accord began to excuse themselves.
>
> "The first said, 'I have bought a field and must go and look at it. Please let me be excused.'
>
> "Another said, 'I have bought five yoke of oxen and am on my way to try them. Please let me be excused.'"

A Zen retreat could be described as a spiritual banquet—with every detail arranged to help the individual get an ever deeper awareness of pure mind, ultimately leading to a sudden awakening to the essential nature of reality. For a Christian, the essential nature of reality is the Divine Reign throughout the whole realm of Heaven and Earth, the Kingdom of Heaven.

Just as Kyudo Roshi said, the best advice for doing *zazen* is written up all over the London subway: "Keep straight on." So Jesus Christ said:

No one who has put his hand to the plough and looks
behind him is fit for the Kingdom of God.

Pure Mind

Pure mind is the path to enlightenment. This emptying or cleaning
of the mind is the necessary precondition or preparation for the
experience of enlightenment. So, for example, in one of the *koans:*

> Once a monk said to Joshu: "I have just entered the mon-
> astery, please give me instructions, Master."
> Joshu said: "Have you had your breakfast?"
> "Yes, I have," replied the monk.
> "Then," said Joshu, "wash your bowls."
> The monk had an insight.

Similarly Sochu Roshi talked about *zazen* as a kind of "body laundry," as a way of cleaning ourselves out, body and mind combined,
to become as clean as a plate or bowl, pristine as a new shirt. Of
course the plate has to be cleaned: you don't want yesterday's left-
overs polluting the taste of the new food. Of course the shirt needs
to be washed. But how do we clean ourselves, get rid of the residue
of old, fixed ideas, the centuries of accumulated cultural conditioning, the years of indoctrination, and the habits of a lifetime?

If you want to take in something new, get fresh ideas, it is a necessary prerequisite to clear out the old, stale attitudes, habits, and
ideas. This is what makes way for the change.

Bearing in mind the initial importance of this pure, clean state of
mind for Zen meditation, it is possible to discern a similar strand of
teaching in the Christian Gospels. Jesus praises the pure in heart,
and throughout early Christian tradition the heart was considered
the deep seat of the mind, the profound feeling-mind, in contrast
to the more superficial intellect. He also used the images of the

bowl and the garments, as well as the image of the light penetrating and illuminating the dark corners of the mind.

> Alas for you that clean the outside of the cup and bowl. Clean first the inside that the outside may be clean as well.

After meditation Christ's own clothes are said to have shone resplendently. And in his stories about the banquet, even though the guests are brought in off the streets and byways, they must be dressed for a wedding.

The radiance of Christians is later compared with that of Moses, whose face was so dazzlingly bright after his experience on Mount Sinai that he had to veil it from the onlookers.

The Kingdom of Heaven

Meditation is not an end in itself; it is the means to a realization. The pivot of Christ's teaching was about the Kingdom of Heaven. The question is this: Was this Kingdom a way of describing a realization of something similar to the enlightenment experience of Zen?

> [Jesus] was asked by the Pharisees when the Kingdom of God was coming, and he answered them by saying: "The Kingdom of God is not coming with signs to be observed. People will not be saying, 'Here it is ' or 'There!' And the reason why is this—the Kingdom of God is within you."

Similarly, Master Hakuin said:

> Where else can you find the buddhas, except in living beings? Not knowing how near the truth is, we seek it

far away—what a pity! We are like the son of a rich man who wandered away among the poor.

Like the experience of enlightenment in Zen, the Kingdom of Heaven is also to be sought now: put first and foremost, before everything else. Forty-eight Zen *koans* have been collected under the title of *The Gateless Gate*. The gates represent the psychological barriers that have to be passed on the way to acquiring Zen wisdom. Similarly, Christ urged his followers to break through barriers:

> "It is indeed an easier thing for a camel to pass through the eye of a needle than for a rich man to enter the King- dom of God."
> "Then who can be saved?" said the people who heard this.
> "What is impossible for men," [Jesus] said, "is possible for God."

Zen realization is something precious, a great treasure. Sochu Roshi named his London Zen building "The Diamond Treasure Mountain" and frequently used the image of handing out treasure. In the Christian literature, the Kingdom is compared to a treasure buried in a field.

> The Kingdom of Heaven is like a merchant looking out for beautiful pearls. He finds one of great value, and goes and sells all he has to buy it.

This suggests something of the dedication required in order to gain entrance into the Kingdom of Heaven. Similarly, in Zen, there is this story:

The Second Patriarch stood in the snow. He cut off his arm and presented it to Bodhidharma crying, "My mind has no peace as yet. I beg you, Master, please pacify my mind."

There is another story in the Zen literature about one master, Gutei Zenji, who cuts off the finger of one of his followers.

And I have already mentioned the story about the novice eager to enter monastic training who had his leg broken in the gates to the monastery.

Again, we can find a strikingly similar example from the teachings of Jesus. Jesus urges his followers to manifest a degree of urgency, sincerity, and firm devotion to practice similar to that which the Second Patriarch communicated to Bodhidharma.

If your hand leads you into evil, cut it off: it is better for you to come into life maimed. If your eye leads you into evil pluck it out: it is better for you to come into the Kingdom of God with one eye.

With these stories in mind, I once suggested to Kyudo Roshi that even if some Western person did manage to cripple himself tying his legs in knots in the full-lotus position, it didn't matter all that much, legs were not so important as all that. "What do you mean?" Kyudo Roshi said: "Legs are not important. What nonsense!" He chuckled, and then said seriously, "Legs are very important."

With regard to the Kingdom of Heaven, Christ said to the circle of his closest followers:

To you the mysteries of the Kingdom are revealed, but to the rest, parables, so that they may hear without understanding.

This suggests that the Gospels themselves only revealed so much of the original teaching—as much as was suitable for the ears of uninitiated beginners. As a result, for a long time it was conjectured that there were other, Secret Gospels with the more complete teachings for those who had been initiated into the mystery of the Kingdom of Heaven. Thus, the more profound aspects of Christian spiritual practice and teaching appeared to be missing from the Gospels as we had them. This was recently confirmed by the discovery of an important letter from Clement of Alexandria, who was born sometime around the year 180. Following is a short extract of Clement's letter, which unequivocally indicates the existence of a set of teachings not included in the canonical Gospels.

> When Peter died as a martyr, Mark came over to Alexandria, bringing both his own notes and those of Peter. Thus he composed a more spiritual Gospel for those who were being perfected. Nevertheless, he did not divulge the things not to be uttered. Dying, he left his composition to the church in Alexandria, where it even yet is most carefully guarded, being read only to those who are being initiated into the great mysteries.
>
> "Not all true things are said to be for all men." For this reason, the Wisdom of God, through Solomon, advises that the light of the truth should be hidden from those who are mentally blind. But we are the "children of light" having been illuminated by the Spirit of the Lord, and "Where the Spirit of the Lord is, there is liberty."

Furthermore, the Secret Gospels include a passage that is striking for another reason altogether:

> Going out of the tomb, they came into the house of the youth, for he was rich. And after six days Jesus told him

what to do and in the evening the youth came to him, and remained with him that night, for Jesus taught him the mystery of the Kingdom of God.

This sounds very like the initiation of Zen, after a six-day *sesshin*, ending with an all-night sitting and a breakthrough.

5 THE IMMEDIATE SEQUEL

From the First Christian Communities
to the Desert Fathers

When Jesus Christ, after his death and resurrection, had been lifted up and a cloud took him out of sight, the Bible tells us:

> [His followers] returned to Jerusalem and went to the upper room where they were staying. All of them with one accord devoted themselves to meditation (the company of persons was in all about a hundred and twenty).
>
> [Ten days later] when the day of Pentecost had come, they were all together in the place and suddenly a sound came from Heaven like a rush of mighty wind, and it filled the house where they were sitting. And there appeared to them tongues as of fire resting on each one of them and they were all filled with the Holy Spirit.

In their subsequent teaching, Jesus' disciples also urge their followers to "meditate without ceasing," as their master did before them.

According to John Cassian who lived from approximately 360–440, the monks of the desert traced their origins, without break, to the first Christian communities.

Just as the Essene communities now seem the likely background for many of the first Christian converts, so it seems more than likely that another group of extremely dedicated Jews living the community life in Egypt must have strongly influenced the first Christian monks or converted to Christianity and became those first Christian monks, bringing with them a spiritual practice and discipline.

The Jewish community near Alexandria was so like the later Christian monastic communities that Eusebius (an early church historian who lived from 265–340) and many others after him, were deceived into thinking that they must have been Christian monks. If it were these very same communities that at some unknown date adopted the kindred spirituality of the early Christians—thereby forming the base of subsequent Christian monasticism—then he was not far wrong. Meanwhile Philo's descriptions of these communities help fill out the early period. Eusebius states:

> In the work he entitled *The Contemplative Life*, Philo lays special emphasis on the renunciation of property, saying that they go outside the walls and make their homes on lonely farms and plantations, well aware that association with men of different ideas is unprofitable. With eager and ardent faith they disciplined themselves to emulate the prophetic way of life. Similarly all who were owners of land or houses, Scripture tells us, sold them and brought the price they fetched and laid them at the Apostles' feet, so that it was distributed to everyone in accordance with individual needs. Having testified to practices very similar to these, Philo goes on:
>
> "The community is to be found in many parts of the world....
>
> "The whole period from dawn to dusk is given up to spiritual discipline.
>
> "They not only practice contemplation... Having first

laid down self-control as the foundation of the soul, they build the other virtues on it. None of them would take food or drink before sundown. Some think of food only once in three days. Others so delight and luxuriate as they feast on wisdom that they scarcely taste food once in six days, having accustomed themselves.

"There are women also who have remained single through their passionate craving for wisdom with which they were so eager to live that they scorned bodily pleasures and set their hearts not on mortal children but on immortal, which only the soul that loves God can bring into the world."

The Righteous Men and Anthony of the Desert

Just as even the Buddha relied on the teaching and transmission of an older ascetic, so Anthony of the Desert relied on the teaching and training of the righteous men—one old man in particular—from whom he learned about the righteous men of old. It may be that this was a line of teachers related to James the Righteous, of Jerusalem. There is some evidence for this, apart from the extract from Cassian that traces the tradition of the Desert Fathers back to the Jerusalem church in an "unbroken" line.

Eusebius describes James, "the Lord's brother," and "the most righteous of men because of the heights of religion which he scaled in his life." And he quotes Hegesippus, who "belonged to the first generation after the apostles":

> Control of the church passed to the apostles, together with the Lord's brother James, whom everyone, from the Lord's time to our own, has called the Righteous, for there were many Jameses, but this one was holy from his birth; he drank no wine or intoxicating liquor and ate

no animal food; no razor came near his head; he did not smear himself with oil.

His garments were of linen. Because of his unsurpassable righteousness, he was called "the Righteous" and "the Bulwark of Righteousness."

Likewise it was said of Anthony:

A righteous idea entered his mind, how the blessed apostles forsook everything, and how the others who succeeded them walked in their footsteps. He was wont to listen to the reading of the scriptures in such wise that not one word would fall to the ground, and henceforth he kept in his mind the remembrance of the commandments which he heard. His food was bread and salt and his drink was water, and in the matter of wine and flesh he declared them to be so superfluous that they ought not to be used even by ordinary monks. He was, moreover, exceedingly careful not to anoint himself with oil, and required young men to distill upon themselves, from their inward minds, the oil of strenuousness.

In this biography, there are a number of things that remind me of stories about the Zen masters, and also of my own experiences with my Zen teachers. Above all there is the emphasis on the very important relationship between an older man and Anthony, which laid the foundations of his spiritual training and set him on the path toward spiritual excellence. It was likened to the relationship of father to son. Anthony, in turn, became the vital link between the experience of past ascetics and the future generation of young monks who flocked to him for instruction. This transmission of the craft of spirituality and its essential inner point, conveyed directly from mind to mind, from one generation to the next, is indispensable in Zen—just as the father is indispensable in the physical realm, or there is no son.

As in Zen, the work of the monk in Anthony's time was strenuous, with no days off. Even the nights were employed. The way Anthony started each day as if he were just a beginner, reminded me of Shunryu Suzuki Roshi's book *Zen Mind, Beginner's Mind*, and the Zen tradition of throwing away great enlightenment experiences. For example, one monk, who had cracked the first *koan* and discovered for himself the limitless depths of "nothing" in Zen, asked his teacher what he thought of his "nothing." "Get rid of it," his teacher said.

In this biography, Anthony seems to make reference to just such a fresh, free mind that had existed from the beginning and was the inner Kingdom of Heaven, pure life.

It was after meditating in a tomb that Anthony had his first important spiritual experience, which left him physically stronger. This made me wonder about the period in the tomb, just before Jesus spends six days and a night initiating his rich young follower into the mysteries of the Kingdom. But it is also reminiscent of Hakuin Zenji meditating in the graveyard, and the importance of death in both Zen meditation and Christian meditation—dying on the mat in Zen, and dying daily with Christ. It seems to be a universal feature of religion that the personal ego must die before the individual can make contact with the powerful forces of the unconscious realm, but in Zen this collective unconscious realm must also be wiped out in order to discover the universal original nature, there from the beginning, without any master or any restriction. Anthony also speaks in terms of the nature of the life that is in us, and the rectitude of life as it was, at its first creation, in the beginning.

The discovery of this true nature affects the body: hard meditation made Anthony's body glow like an angel of light. Another of the Desert Fathers was said to have been able to read by the light of his own aura. The bodies of my own Zen teachers seem to have glowed like fire at times. After twenty years Anthony reportedly had not aged, and the stories of the Desert Fathers spoke of the "openness of face" that was acquired through meditation. Similarly Sochu Roshi used to say at the end of *sesshin*: "Everyone—baby face. Nice face." He advised us to look in the mirror.

Anthony was used to much hard labor and commented, "If a man doth not work, he shall not eat." Like Anthony, Zen monks also do manual work every day. There is a Zen story that tells of monks who, out of love and consideration, wanted their master to conserve his energy. They once hid his gardening tools, but then the master just refused to eat, saying, like Anthony, "No work, no food."

But the real work for Zen monks, as for Christian monks, was meditation: the Greek word for monk (*hesychast*) means "keeping still." As Sochu Roshi used to say, "Stay at home." No need for journeys by land or sea—just sit and work directly upon the mind, the inner life.

The ordeals of Anthony's life were much more arduous and extreme than a Zen *sesshin*, or even eight such *sesshin*s per year as the monks do when training; but if the same goal could be obtained with less extreme measures, then it would be so much the better for everyone. In other disciplines too, it is certainly true that the pioneers often had to take extreme measures that were not required later: consider the centuries of human effort leading to the first airplane that could fly, for example. So it is possible that success in spiritual practice might be no exception to this general principle. We can all benefit from the hardships and accumulated experience of previous generations.

The important question is whether the means are effective—not how arduous they are. What *does* matter is if they lead to the same results, the same realization, the same transformation of mind and body. Perhaps the real difference between Anthony's time and now lies in the fact that the methods have become more refined and the goal more accessible.

6 THE LINE OF CHRISTIAN SPIRITUAL MASTERS

The Investigation Continued

Over the years I began to find more and more evidence of a Christian tradition of pure meditation (pure prayer) that closely resembled Zen. There was the same insistence on stillness, especially remaining in the monastic cell, in order to empty and purify the mind. There was the same emphasis on the battle against wandering thoughts—and all this in order to experience the Kingdom of Heaven here and now—an experience with clear parallels to the enlightenment experience in Zen.

The pure meditation tradition in Christianity was not just a flash in the pan but lasted a full fourteen centuries. Nor was it practiced by an esoteric group on the sidelines of Christianity—the practice was consistently attributed to Christ himself and passed down master-to-master in communities founded solely for the purpose of continuing the tradition. Most of these spiritual masters were ranked as great saints, some as Teachers (then called "Doctors") of the Church, and one ranked with John the Apostle and only three or four others as one of the Divines of the Orthodox Church. In Zen, it is traditional to know the whole list of who-enlightened-whom back to Buddha, and the whole list was recited daily, and often learned by heart. In the case of Christianity, the following might be included in a short list of Christian Spiritual Masters:

Jesus Christ

John the Baptist

Mary Magdalene

James the Righteous (first century)

Anthony of the Desert, called the Great (third century)

Evagrios the Solitary (fourth century)

John Cassian (fourth–fifth centuries)

The master of the works attributed to Denys of Athens
(c. fifth century)

Maximos the Confessor (seventh century)

Hesychios the Priest (eighth or ninth century)

Simeon the New Theologian (tenth century)

Gregory of Palamas (fourteenth century)

The master who wrote *The Cloud of Unknowing* (fourteenth
century)

As a result of the great schism in the church in the eleventh century, few Christians on the Western Roman side of the rift would
know much about the important Christian teachers of Eastern
Orthodoxy—even if they studied theology, and even if they were
monks. With the reconciliation of the Pope and the Eastern Patriarch in the 1960s, there may be room for gradual change, and
Roman Catholics may become increasingly familiar with Christianity's roots in the Middle East. As a result, it has taken a special
inquiry on my part to discover this evidence and present it to Western Christians. But by contrast, it was the teaching held in the highest regard by the flourishing Byzantine church, where new teachers
often referred to the line of great names before them who were
responsible for upholding this core authentic teaching, which was
finally collected in the eighteenth century by St. Nikodimos of
the Holy Mountain and St. Makarios of Corinth in the definitive
edition that they called the *Philokalia (Love of Spiritual Excellence)*. This
collection of Christian teaching was prized by the Greek and Russian

Orthodox Churches as an anthology second only to the Bible in importance for the practicing Christian; and its importance lies most especially in the instructions it contains about how to meditate—for which not even the Bible itself is a better source of information. The *Philokalia* is the authoritative Christian teaching on meditation.

Right (or virtuous) action is a very important part of Christianity, but right action proceeds directly from the right state of mind, and pure meditation is what has the most direct effect on the mind. One does not choose between meditation and action. One must both meditate *and* act—the one complements the other. Pure Christianity—that is the Christianity of pure meditation—if practiced properly, cultivates the mind, discovers its own deep inner resources of wisdom, and acts in accordance with them. If the following pages deal almost exclusively with the Christian teaching about meditation, it is not because the active side of Christian life was considered unimportant by the writers from whom I quote; on the contrary, it was considered of utmost importance. But it was their equally important teaching about the hard activity of controlling the mind by meditation that has been neglected. The activity itself has been marred, and has frequently proven inadequate when not backed by sufficiently profound psychological training.

Therefore, it is reasonable to hope that if those modern Christians who are sincere, well-meaning, and active in the service of their neighbor, also return to the practice of meditation, then the fruit of their active work will be all the more abundant. And indeed some of the most effective Christians (such as Mother Teresa, Abbé Pierre, or Lord Soper) have put considerable emphasis on the need for meditation alongside activity.

Not only is it false to set up a choice between either meditation or action, it is also false even to put meditating in a separate category from activity. Pure meditation (especially *zazen*) is an intense activity that makes very considerable demands on the physical body while nurturing the living spirit. It is work on the whole individual.

From the Third to Seventh Centuries: The Desert Fathers

If the teaching of Jesus Christ centered on meditation leading to a change of heart (a renewed, pure mind) culminating in the direct experience of the Kingdom of Heaven, then the Desert Fathers must be regarded as the next great teachers of authentic mainstream Christianity, in direct line with the first Christian communities. Their whole way of life, their sayings, and their spiritual powers all tend to support this view.

The Desert Fathers provide the link between the first-century Christians and the monastic movement in the Orthodox tradition, with its great centers of spiritual training in St. Katherine's and other monasteries in Sinai, the Stoudion Monastery in Byzantium, and the monasteries on Mount Athos. The comparative stability of the Eastern branch of the Roman Empire, which fell to the Turks a thousand years after the fall of Rome, may have favored the flourishing spiritual continuity there.

John Cassian hazarded an attempt to transplant this line of spirituality into the West, founding the monastery of St. Victor near Marseilles, which numbered 5,000 monks at one time, but in the preface to his *Conferences*, he was only too aware of the difficulties of his task. He expressed the hope that by growing acquaintance with the masters of the desert, brought about through his book, his monks might gain additional resources to find the difficult way to the Kingdom of Heaven. Cassian hoped that they might learn to follow the rule of the solitary's life, taught by the examples of the Desert Fathers who preserved this ancient tradition.

The Wit and Wisdom of the Christian Fathers of Egypt, translated by E.A. Wallis Budge, speaks clearly of this path:

The perfection of the monk ariseth from spiritual conduct, and spiritual conduct is acquired from conduct of the heart, and purity of heart ariseth from the conduct of the mind, and the conduct of the mind from meditation which is unceasing. But unceasing meditation and the contendings with thoughts have no opportunity for existence without silence and solitariness.

The same book offers sound advice on dealing with the arising of thoughts during meditation:

A brother said: "I have very many thoughts, O father, whereby I am vexed." The old man took him out into the air and said: "Spread out thy skirt and catch the winds," and the brother said, "I cannot do this." The old man said: "Neither canst thou prevent thy thoughts from coming, but it belongeth to thee to stand up against them."

And:

A certain brother vexed an old man several times by saying unto him, "What shall I do in respect of the thoughts of all sorts and kinds which go through me?" The old man answered: "Thou art like unto a stagnant pool. Why canst thou not rather be like unto a spring which never fails? Patient persistence is constancy, constancy is life, and life is the Kingdom."

These two images of standing firm against the rush of thoughts—sitting like a mountain with the thoughts pouring past like wind, and persistently flowing with the breath, leaving the thoughts behind like sediment—may sound contradictory, but they are two sides to a coin. One image is referring to the persistent stillness of the body, which stills the mind, and the other to the constant flow of the breath, calm and persistent, which purifies the mind.

Consider the following:

> Abbot Poeman asked Abbot Joseph: "What shall I do when the passions rise up against me wishing to make me quake?" The old man said: "Let them shake thee, and strive with them." But to another brother who asked the same old man the same question, he spoke differently: "Thou shalt not let them draw nigh to thee in any way, but cut them off quickly."

The stillness, the battle with the thoughts, the persistence in skilled spiritual work are all very similar in Christian meditation and Zen. As with Zen, the communal life certainly precedes the solitary life, but considering that the turning point for the first Christian community came when a hundred and twenty of them were persevering in meditation with one accord, it is surprising how little value is placed on silent meditation in groups—which I feel is one of the great strengths of Zen. For all my investigations, I have found no record of anything equivalent to a Zen *sesshin* (except those ten days before Pentecost) where the numbers of like-minded people, persevering in the same spiritual work, generate an extraordinary spiritual strength that enables each of them to accomplish what each could never manage on his or her own. It is possible that it was not mentioned because it was so overwhelmingly obvious— such an ordinary everyday part of communal life. Of course the whole point of the communal life and the solitary life was the same: a still and silent life that stilled and silenced the mind. There is a story that could support this view:

> They used to say about a certain monk who lived in a monastery of the brotherhood, that although he kept

frequent vigil and meditated, he was neglectful about meditating with the congregation. And one night there appeared unto him a glorious pillar of brilliant light from the place where the brethren were congregated, and it reached up into the heavens; and he saw a small spark which flew about the pillar, and sometimes it shone brightly and sometimes it was extinguished. And whilst he was wondering at the vision, it was explained to him: "The pillar which thou seest is the meditation of the many brethren which are gathered together. If thou would live, perform that which it is customary to perform with the brethren, and then, if thou wishes to do so, and art able to meditate separately, do so."

No more is said about what was customary, but this light or fire is on other occasions associated with the life of pure meditation, as well as with the pure mind that was the immediate aim of that form of prayer. Consider the following:

Abbot Lot went to Abbot Joseph and said: "As far as lieth in my power I cleanse my thoughts, what more can I do?" Then the old man stood up and spread his hands toward heaven, and his fingers were like unto ten lamps of fire, and he said unto him, "If thou wishest, let the whole of thee be like unto fire."

And this:

They used to say that the face of the old man Sylvanus shone so brightly with the glorious splendor which he had received from God that no man was able to look upon it with his eyes wide open.

This visible light occasionally manifests the clear, pure mind, cultivated by pure meditation, and often only accomplished fully in old age. Regarding purity, *The Wit and Wisdom of the Christian Fathers of Egypt* offers this:

> Purity consists of being oblivious of various kinds of knowledge, so that being wholly free from them, a man arrives at a state of natural simplicity and integrity which he possessed at first.

And regarding the need for meditation:

> Abbot Anthony said to certain brethren: "It is said in the Gospel, 'If a man smite thee on one cheek, turn the other also.'" They said unto him, "We cannot do this." Abbot Anthony said, "If ye cannot turn the other cheek, continue to be smitten on the one cheek." They said to him, "And this we cannot do." And the old man said, "If ye cannot do even this, do not pay back blows in return for the smiting which ye have received." "We cannot even do this." Then the old man said unto his disciples: "If ye cannot do this and ye are unable to do the other things, meditation is necessary forthwith."

Only by purifying the heart—the depths of the feeling-mind and the seat of passion—can we free ourselves from our particular egoistic reactions to which we are tethered by long conditioning. The storm of the ego is always on the surface, but in the depths of the mind there is unlimited peace. In the above account, the instructions for how to react come with the method for achieving the desired result: meditation. Without the method, the mere instruction is likely to prove ineffectual or even counterproductive.

There is a Zen story in which a great Chinese scholar of Buddhism heard about the reputation of a Zen master in the south of China. He took the hazardous journey of thousands of miles and found the man living up in a tree. The scholar asked him what wisdom he had to impart. The old man replied, "Do good and avoid evil." The scholar was furious, pointing out that any child of four could have told him that. "True," said the master, "any child can say it, but there's many a white-haired old man who still hasn't done it." Yet Zen provides the means to achieve this—controlling the individual ego, from which all action proceeds.

One of the most renowned of the Desert Fathers, Simeon the Stylite (ca. 390–459), lived on the top of a pillar for thirty-six years in the Syrian desert after twenty years of training in various monasteries and hermitages. The top of the pillar was twelve-feet square—four times the size of a Zen mat. Even more than Anthony of the Desert, Simeon the Stylite remains the most striking image of the authentic Christian ideal of keeping still. Like Anthony, and similar to the tree-dwelling Zen master, Simeon was consulted by people of all ranks from all parts of the Christian Empire, including emperors.

As with Zen, the wisdom of the desert has nothing to do with the learning that can be gained through books. For Anthony, the pure mind was the source of books, not the other way around, and as a result of sitting still and discovering its reaches, his wisdom exceeded that of the Greek philosophers who came to him. As Cassian notes, the wisdom acquired is not rugged or unsophisticated, as people might think if it were only the simple villagers who practiced meditation. But when more sophisticated people practice spiritual discipline and acquire spiritual knowledge, they put it in sophisticated terms, and in this way the spiritual life can be made appealing to all types.

From the Orthodox Monks and Cassian
to the Fourteenth Century

There was considerable overlap between the founding of the great monasteries of the Eastern Orthodox branch of the Christian Church and the Desert Fathers. The tradition was so consistent, with notable teachers and spiritual masters in every century, that it is reasonable to assume that there was some form of strict succession, or direct transmission—master to disciple without break—although only the more remarkable of such relationships are recorded in detail. Nevertheless, as in Zen, great importance was attached to this relationship, even though not each spiritual generation has been preserved by name in quite the same way.

With a good teacher anyone can follow the difficult spiritual path. Whereas without one, even the most spiritually gifted might not get very far. The process of learning, practicing, and finally teaching is vital. In later times, when good teachers were getting scarce, it was advised that the young monk be thoroughly familiar with the books by the former generations of spiritual teachers, so as to ensure that the teaching he was getting corresponded with the old tradition; but it was still essential to find a teacher. So by force of circumstances the monks came increasingly to treasure the written testimony of the ancient fathers, both of the desert and of the monasteries.

The *Philokalia* contained everything of practical value for the monk or hermit trying to practice the spiritual life; yet the compilers of the *Philokalia* end by emphasizing that the instructions are for all Christians—not just hermits and monks.

One of the earliest and most influential teachers of the practical methods of stillness was Evagrios the Solitary, born circa 345. His teachers included Makarios, the founder-father of the complex of monasteries and hermitages in the region of Sketis in the Egyptian desert, and also another Makarios of Alexandria. He, in turn, was the teacher of John Cassian. Of stillness, Evagrios the Solitary said:

> If a jar of wine is left in the same place for a long time, the wine in it becomes clear, settled, and fragrant. But if it is moved about, the wine becomes turbid and dull, tainted throughout by the lees.

And regarding meditation:

> I shall say again what I have said elsewhere: blessed is the mind completely free from forms during meditation.

Denys of Athens left behind wisdom that formed the conceptual foundation of Christian teachers who would come after him. For example, St. Maximos quoted him extensively with regard to Divine realities:

> The mind possesses the faculty to perceive spiritual realities: it possesses the capacity for a union that transcends its nature and unites it with what is beyond its natural scope. It is through this union that Divine realities are apprehended, by virtue of the fact that we entirely transcend ourselves.

And with regard to the unifying power of enlightenment, St. Maximos says:

> Just as ignorance divides those who are deluded, so the presence of spiritual light draws together and unites those whom it enlightens. It makes them perfect and brings them back to what really exists; converting them from a multiplicity of opinions it unites their various fantasies

into one simple, true, and pure spiritual knowledge, and fills them with a single unifying light.

Another of Maximos' teachings echoes the Zen idea of "dying on the mat":

> When the intellect dies while in that supreme state of meditation, it is separated from all conceptual images. If it does not die such a death it cannot be with God.

Just as Maximos the Confessor selected and passed on what he found of greatest value in the teaching of Denys, so John Cassian's chief aim was to impart to Europe all he had learned from his spiritual masters in the Egyptian desert. His *Conferences* are possibly the most coherent account of their teaching. He founded two very large monastic communities (one for men and one for women) for the practice of a life centered around meditation, but described their practice as a mere primer compared with the spiritual training of the Desert Masters.

Benedict—the founder of the flourishing Benedictine order—in turn described his own writings as being only for beginners on the spiritual path compared with the *Institutes* and *Conferences* of Cassian, which were to be read daily. Benedict left little time for and put little emphasis on the stillness that led to the inner silence of pure meditation—the way to a pure mind, and the Kingdom of Heaven. For example, Benedict wrote: "Meditation should be short and pure unless perhaps it is prolonged under the inspiration of divine grace. In community however, meditation should always be brief." During Lent the monks were urged to add something to the measure of it by way of private meditation. Though not emphasized by Benedict, this mention of meditation in community clearly testifies to a recognized practice of pure prayer in groups (as in Zen). Benedict finishes by making it clear that this is only the beginning of the spiritual work, and "anyone hastening on to the perfection of monastic life" or wanting "to set out for the loftier summits," should seek the teachings of the fathers that Cassian's works elucidate. Cassian's monks appear to have been among the founding fathers of Celtic monasticism, which was so influential in introducing Christianity to much of Northern Europe. For a long time, Celtic monasticism preserved strong ties with the Eastern Orthodox branch of the Church.

Kyudo Roshi has frequently urged his Zen followers to make "hard effort," saying, "If thoughts come, don't follow them." In like manner, Cassian passed on the teaching:

> It is impossible for the mind not to be troubled by thoughts. But if we exert ourselves, it is within our power either to accept them and give them our attention, or to expel them. The amending of our mind is also within the power of our choice and effort. When we meditate wisely and continually, thoughts diminish and find no place.

Cassian himself received counsel from an old man named Serenus regarding his own professed inability to meditate:

> It is dangerous to jump to a conclusion looking only at your own weakness instead of basing your judgment on the character and value of the practice itself. The mind is ever-shifting and 'museth on many things', until accustomed by long practice and daily use—in which you say you have toiled without result—it persists in the state and condition to which it aspires. We ought then certainly to ascribe this wandering inclination of our heart to our own laziness or carelessness. It lies in our power.

Cassian reveals another similarity in the Christian and Zen monastic traditions: the ordeal before being allowed to enter a monastery. Cassian says:

> One who seeks to be admitted to the discipline of the monastery is never received before he gives—by lying outside the doors for ten days or even longer—an evidence of his perseverance and desire, as well as patience.
>
> He should meditate so that he may be completely emptied...and become a spiritual world, splendid and vast.

This self-emptying is very important both in Zen and Christian teaching. Christ emptied himself of his Divinity ("became *Mu*," as Yamada Koun Roshi suggests) and shared our humanity, so that we, by emptying ourselves of our humanity, might share his Divinity. Cassian reminds us where this Divinity is to be found:

> All the treasures of wisdom and spiritual knowledge are hidden in our hearts. This is the treasure hidden in the field—of your heart.

He also elucidates what is meant by the Kingdom of Heaven:

> The Kingdom of Heaven consists in possessing an inviolate and pre-eternal knowledge of created things through perceiving their inner essences. It concerns the consummation of created things.

Another master in the Christian tradition was Hesychios the Priest, who lived in the eighth or ninth century, and is not well known apart from his clear concise writings, which are especially recommended by the compilers of the *Philokalia*. Hesychios writes:

The mind's great gain from stillness is this: all the sins which formerly beat upon the mind as thoughts and which, once admitted by the mind, were turned into outward acts, are now cut off by mental watchfulness.

Similarly in Zen, Hakuin declared that those who had practiced *zazen* for just one sitting would see all their evil actions and thoughts erased—"nowhere will they find evil paths."

In either the ninth or tenth century lived a master known as Philotheos of Sinai. Philotheos counsels vigilance, saying:

At every hour and moment let us guard the mind with all diligence from thoughts that obscure the soul's mirror; for in that mirror Jesus Christ, the wisdom and power of God the Father, is luminously reflected. And let us unceasingly seek the Kingdom of Heaven inside our mind: the seed, the pearl, the leaven. Indeed if we cleanse the eye of the mind, we will find all things hidden within us. This is why our Lord Jesus Christ said that the Kingdom of Heaven is within us, indicating that Divinity dwells in our minds.

The state of the mind is central to Zen. Direct work on the mind is crucial. This may be the ultimate point: nothing else is going to change except the state of your mind. Zen practice, like pure prayer, should be real; it should have a beneficial and noticeable effect on everyday life. Christ and his followers in this hard spiritual tradition also taught about this interrelationship.

Simeon the New Theologian (949–1022) is especially important for Christian tradition because of the emphasis and clarity he brought to the matter of the master-to-novice relationship. In Zen, the relationship between the enlightened *roshi* (literally "old teacher") and the young monk or lay person is vital to ensuring the transmission of spiritual truth from one spiritual generation to the next. The slow process of imparting that truth is what transforms the youth into a master, and this is the only guarantee that the teaching continues in a pure, unadulterated form.

The Christian masters in the deserts of Egypt and Syria, and in the monasteries of Sinai and Byzantium, similarly appear to have transmitted their teachings in an unbroken line up to the time of Simeon. Cassian's work offers the Desert Fathers' comments on the need for a teacher, and seems to provide support for the existence of a transmission line:

> Whatever man is desirous to attain skill in any art, unless he observes the rules and orders of the best masters of that work or science, is indulging in a vain hope to reach by idle wishes any similarity to those whose pains and diligence he avoids copying.

The Gospels seem almost to have taken for granted the important master-to-disciple relationship between Jesus Christ and his followers. They also stressed that the disciple must pass on what he himself has learned.

In Christian tradition the master was often referred to as *geron,* the Greek for "old man," and later translated into the Russian as *staretz,* and they seem to have been used as the equivalent of *roshi* in Zen. My own Zen teacher, Sochu Roshi, lived very close to his first teacher, Gempo Roshi, washing his clothes for him and cooking his food.

In the case of Simeon the New Theologian, we have his own vivid account of his relationship with his master (also called Simeon, of the Stoudion monastery in Byzantium) and the value he placed on it. He compared spiritual fatherhood with physical fatherhood:

As children born according to the flesh are neither begotten nor born without a father, so to be born from above is impossible for anyone who does not have the Spirit from those who themselves have been born from above. And as the fleshly father causes fleshly children to be born, so a spiritual man renders spiritual those who want to become his true spiritual sons.

If then a disciple is his teacher's spiritual child, a person who is seeking ought by all means to seek one who himself has had a spiritual birth.

It is plainly true that some people are more spiritually endowed than others and get to the essence more quickly. Yet, one must strive to experience pure mind and discover the Kingdom, whether it takes a long time or a short time. In either case, the proximity of a teacher who passes on this wisdom, directly, mind to mind, seems to be essential. But so is continued spiritual work. Having received the spiritual treasure as a gift from his teacher without particular toil or payment, Simeon nonetheless taught diligence:

On this warfare against thoughts by attention and meditation hangs the life and death of the soul. If by means of attention, we keep meditation pure, we make progress; if we have no attention to keep it pure but leave it unprotected, it becomes soiled with bad thoughts and we remain futile failures...

He who does not have attention in himself and does not guard his mind, cannot become pure in heart and so cannot see God. If you wish also to learn how it should be done, I will tell you of this.

Before all else you should have freedom from all cares, a clear conscience, and the absence of passionate attachment. Keep your attention within yourself—not in your head, but in your heart. Keep your mind there, trying by every possible means to find the place where the heart is, in order that your mind should constantly abide there. Wrestling thus, the mind will find the place of the heart. From that moment onward, from whatever side a thought may appear, the mind immediately chases it away before it has had time to enter. As to other results that usually come from this work, you will learn them from your own experience.

The line of Christian masters teaching meditation as a path to the Kingdom of Heaven continues up until the fourteenth century. Gregory of Palamas (ca. 1296–1359) taught:

Monks should lead the mind inside the body and hold it there. It is not out of place to teach even beginners to keep attention in themselves and to accustom themselves to introduce the mind within, through breathing. No one who thinks rightly would dissuade those who have not yet attained pure meditation from using certain methods to lead the mind into itself. In those who have not long undertaken this work, the mind often jumps out, so that they have at once to bring it back; in those who are not practiced in this work, the mind again slips away, since it is extremely mobile and hard to hold by attention to sin-gleness of pure meditation. Hence some advise them to refrain from breathing fast, but to restrain their breath somewhat, so that together with their breath they may also hold the mind inside, until, with God's help through training, they make it strong enough to concentrate upon one thing. However this restraining of breath naturally follows attention of mind: if one meditates deeply, the breath goes in and out slowly, especially in those who are silent in body and spirit. For these suspend the movements of the soul in relation to all movements of the body, which are in our control...

If "the kingdom of God is within you," would not the man who so zealously tries to chase his mind out from within find himself also outside the Kingdom of Heaven?

And furthermore, Gregory speaks eloquently on meditation and the pure mind:

> Acquiring god-like virtues does not effect Divine union; it is intense meditation by its holy action that accomplishes the soaring of man to God and union with Him; for in its essence meditation is the union of intelligent beings with their Creator. The single mind remains wholly enclosed in itself and in God, tasting the spiritual joy that flows from within. The single mind returns to itself, and rises through itself to God. When a man abides in this collected state of mind, curbing his volatile thoughts by intense effort of self-constraint, he meets with the ineffable. To bring the mind to this state is perhaps not so difficult, but to remain long in this state, which gives birth to something indescribable, is exceedingly difficult. The work on any other virtue is easy compared with it. This is why many, by refusing the straightness of the virtue of meditation, fail to acquire the spaciousness of the gifts; while those who endure it are granted the strength to undertake all things, since it makes the difficult easy.
>
> What is called mind is also activity of mind. Mind is the power that in the Scriptures is also called "heart." This power of the mind is the most important of our powers. In those who practice meditation, the action of mind is

easily purified. It may be that through special attention and diligence, some action of a man's mind proves temporarily pure, and he acquires some measure of enlightenment or mental illumination. If in consequence he considers himself purified he will delude himself. If he does not puff himself up with a measure of, as it were, accidental purity, then it will help him see more clearly and help him find effective means through meditation to reach the true, perfect and stable purity of heart and mind.

From the Fifteenth Century to the Present Day in the Eastern Orthodox Branch of Christianity

From the evidence—of which I have presented a bare outline—it would be hard to dispute that a strong line of Christian spiritual teachers carried the teaching of Christ himself and the first Christian communities right through to the end of the fourteenth century. The communities and hermits to the south—in Egypt and the Sinai, in Syria and Palestine itself—and north around Constantinople and on the holy mountain of Athos, were spiritually united. The records show that teachers traveled from one part to another, bringing the direct person-to-person transmission to areas in a state of comparative decadence.

But after the fourteenth century, if the line held at all, it became a fine thread—a vestige of its former self, hard to trace through the centuries that followed. A refined and polished spiritual tradition depends on support from temporal power, whether in ancient Egypt or China or the Eastern Christian Empire; and the collapse of the Byzantine Empire in 1453—when Constantinople fell to the Turks—must certainly have affected the Christian communities. Although the Turks employed a policy of religious tolerance and made a special treaty with the monks of Mount Athos, the fact that the monks were no longer an integral part of a thriving Christian empire inevitably limited their sphere of influence, which must ultimately have affected their spirituality. Such matters are not easy to assess from this distance in time.

But if it takes a spiritual father to make a spiritual son, then some thin thread of spiritual transmission may have continued to initiate Nicodemus of the Holy Mountain (1748–1809), who once more collected the most valuable writings of the ancient fathers for anyone trying to practice in that tradition. His *Philokalia* was translated into Russian, and the great spiritual revival in Russia is frequently attributed to this book. But, in my experience, a book alone is not capable of such a spiritual revival if unaided by the person carrying the book. The most famous of the Russian *staretz* was Seraphim of Zarov, but it was the thriving monastery at Optino under Abbot Makarios that attracted the attention of Dostoevsky and Tolstoy (who was at a railway station on his way there when he died), as Mount Athos, in this century, attracted Nikos Kazantzakis.

In the West, from Cassian to the Present Day

The Western branch of Christianity has clung obstinately to the widely held idea that spirituality, in contrast with any other aspect of life on earth, is a matter of special gifts ("grace"), each occurrence of which is a spontaneous occurrence—a freak intervention by Heaven. This is never quite so explicitly stated, but the idea lurks there nonetheless. Moreover, the antecedents of each sporadic appearance of some vigorous form of spirituality are largely ignored. The occurrences are so diverse and apparently so unconnected that I suppose the possibility cannot be entirely ruled out that each one of the latter Western masters (if they are to be counted as genuine spiritual masters at all) found his own way by trial and error and personal struggle without a spiritual father to guide him.

But this seems the least likely of the various possible solutions. For one thing, there is a certain consistency about the teaching, which seems to link it with the mainstream teaching of the Eastern Orthodox tradition. And that in turn brings up the very real possibility of continued contact with that teaching and those teachers, at least up to the time of the definite break between East and West in 1054—when the original Orthodox Church of the eastern Mediterranean was anathematized by the officialdom of Rome—a ban that was only lifted in the mid-1960s. It is also possible that the spiritual training and methods of Eastern Christianity could have survived for several centuries past the split, unacknowledged by the Western Church. Another possibility is that the strong tradition brought straight from the Egyptian desert by Cassian was in fact transmitted from one generation of spiritual masters to the next, still fairly widely diffused until the end of the fourteenth century.

To uncover the connections, if possible at all, would be a prodigious scholarly task—unearthing original early documents in many languages, looking only for the who-taught-whom. The clue may lie in the Celtic Church as initiated by one of Cassian's masters. The so-called "Augustinian Order," widely diffused Christian hermits and communities, may also offer insight.

Directly from this Augustinian Order came the great Abbey of St. Victor outside Paris, which was affiliated with the Canons of St. Victor at Marseilles. One is led to speculate that the Abbey of St. Victor may have been spiritually descended from Cassian's great monastery of St. Victor in the same place a few centuries earlier. This new Abbey of St. Victor was rebuilt from ruins by William of Champeaux. It gave spiritual birth to the masters from England and Brittany—among whom is Richard of St. Victor, whose writings one writer, Enomiya-Lassalle, has compared with Zen.

Enomiya-Lassalle has also pointed out detailed comparisons between Zen and the anonymously written *Cloud of Unknowing* (from the fourteenth century), which seems, more than any other work, to suggest a continuity of transmission with the ancient Eastern tradition of spirituality. It is true that he relies on the writings of the monks of St. Victor and on those attributed to St. Denys of Athens, but it is by no means one of those lifeless regurgitations of other people's work. It is generally thought (from the language and content) that *The Cloud of Unknowing* was written by a monk from the north of England, where Celtic spirituality had been very strong a few centuries earlier.

Consider the following from *The Cloud of Unknowing*:

> For those who practice this form of meditation, there is no prior help to be gained from reading or sermons, or thinking about anything whatever.

In Rinzai Zen, the first and most important *koan* that students sit with is called "Master Joshu's *Mu*." The *Mumonkan* introduces this *koan* as follows:

> A monk asked Master Joshu, "Does a dog have buddha-nature?" Joshu answered, "*Mu*."

Literally, *Mu* means "nothing." Students are told to be *Mu*, to practice *Mu* ceaselessly night and day. This *koan* dates from the eighth century A.D., yet the instructions for practicing it, as handed down in the Rinzai Zen school, are echoed strikingly in the following passage from *The Cloud of Unknowing*:

> Another man might tell you to withdraw into yourself—and he would be saying what is absolutely right and true. But I do not care to do so because I fear a physical interpretation of what is said. What I will say is this: See that in no sense you withdraw into yourself. And briefly I do not want you to be outside or above, behind or beside

yourself either. You will say, "Where am I to be? Nowhere according to you." And you will be quite right. "Nowhere" is where I want you. Make it your business to see that your spirit is tied to nothing. And though your natural mind can now find "nothing" to feed on, do not give up but work vigorously on that nothing.

The Cloud of Unknowing goes on to add the following advice on the practice of meditation in the early stages:

The vigorous working of your imagination, which is always so active when you set yourself to this blind meditation, must be suppressed. Unless you suppress it, it will suppress you. Make up your mind therefore to put down all reflections, holy and attractive though they be. It is more worthwhile that you have this blind outreaching to the cloud of unknowing than that you should gaze on angels and saints in heaven and hear the happy music of the blessed.

And this on the struggle against egocentric awareness:

As often as in his purity of heart a man would know the true awareness of God, he finds his awareness held and filled with the lump of himself. Yet in all this he does not want to cease existing: that would be madness. Though he continues longing to be free of its awareness, he wants very much to go on in existence, and he gives heartfelt thanks for this precious gift.

This "lump of the self" mentioned in The Cloud is also strikingly similar to a description of the Zen practice of sitting with Mu. Zen describes the experience like this: "It is as if you have a red-hot ball of iron in your throat, and you can neither swallow it nor spit it out." The iron must be cooled and whittled by the breath, until it is finally dissolved, digested, and absorbed. Both the "lump of the self" and the "iron ball" are images of the struggle against the egocentric view that continues even after one has glimpsed a greater reality. And on dealing with this struggle, *The Cloud* has this advice:

> Work with eager enjoyment, rather than with brute force. Violent strainings of the animal heart are inseparable from a materialistic and physical outlook. Remember your manners. Do not snatch at what you want like some famished dog. I would suggest that you do all you can to cloak your great and ungoverned spiritual rage.

But after the fourteenth century, and *The Cloud of Unknowing*, it becomes increasingly difficult to trace the course of Christian meditation in the West. It is as if this fundamental Christian teaching went underground. The art of pure meditation gradually became an esoteric teaching, and became increasingly unknown to lay Christians. Where could one go for basic instructions? Where was this core Christian practice to be found? How could it be learned and passed on? There were instances, times, and places where pure contemplative prayer was taught and practiced—but they seem to have been few and far between. For example, the Christians in Spain seem to have upheld the importance of meditation (alongside Islamic and Jewish mystics) longer than those in other parts of Western Christendom. St. Ignatius Loyola with his companion St. Francis Xavier left the Jesuits in their wake, and St. Theresa of Avila with St. John of the Cross founded the reformed Carmelites. Later still, in the seventeenth century, Mère Angélique and the Jansenists at Port-Royal lived for a short while by the rules and wisdom of the Desert Fathers, as expounded in John Cassian's clear account.

However, the mainstream tradition of this latter era seems more commonly to have left the individual to find his or her own way along the intricate paths of the interior spiritual life of pure prayer. Those few individuals who did come to this "mystical" or "simple" prayer did so toward the end of their lives. Furthermore, pure prayer was widely considered the special prerogative of certain exceptional spirits only. But this was not what Jesus taught his young followers when he urged them to watch and meditate through all hours of the night, often in the company of others.

The ability to groom a successor who would then pass on the torch seems to have been completely lost in these latter centuries. St. Ignatius Loyola and St. Theresa of Avila both left organizations behind, but not a line of true successors. There is danger in letting an organization take the place of the master-to-student teaching. In the long run an organization can never be a substitute for this personal teaching. This personal transmission of the teaching—so clearly described in the cases of Simeon of Stoudion and Simeon the Divine— had been common practice for many Christian centuries. But now, this personal transmission his ceased to be a part of the Christian tradition.

Nonetheless, some individuals have reached profound depths of prayer. I have met some of them—men and women of prayer—and very impressive they were. But not one of them ever took me aside and said: "Look, this is how it is done. If you want this, I can help you get it." But this is precisely what my Zen teacher did! And that is the most fundamental difference between the open craft of Buddhist teaching available to all, and the closed shop of Christian meditation during the past few centuries.

A Break in the Chain of Christian Transmission

Jesus Christ appears to have based his teaching on the spiritual practice of meditation—both by his example of frequent meditation (often all night, and at least once for a sustained forty-day period) and by his express command to his followers to "meditate cease-lessly." His teachings were clearly intended to lead his followers to the experience, here and now, of the Kingdom of Heaven—the recurrent central theme of his message. The exact nature of this practice seems to have been kept carefully guarded to prevent dilu-tion and corruption, and disclosed only gradually during the process of initiation.

But from the consistent line of practice and teaching among his followers, we can learn more about the details of the practice Jesus taught. And from this, it appears that pure meditation without thought or object—practiced in order to achieve pure mind or "purity of heart" and thereby enter the Kingdom of Heaven—is the one authentic strand of Christian spiritual practice that can be traced through at least fourteen centuries back to Jesus Christ and John the Baptist.

Along the way there have been many accretions and additions to this central practice, but none of them were given the same weight as those taught by the founder of Christianity himself. There is room for many strands of Christian practice, but we must be wary that they don't occlude Jesus Christ's main point, and obscure the essential work of entering the Kingdom of Heaven in this very life.

Up until the end of the fourteenth century, pure prayer was the flourishing spiritual practice of Christianity, still true to the intentions of its founder. Even when meditation wasn't practiced by the ecclesiastical establishment, it was largely recognized as the authentic Christian teaching. For the most part, the ecclesiastical authorities canonized the important masters of the Christian way of meditation, and, in the case of Gregory of Palamas, honored him further with the title of Doctor, and in the case of Simeon the New Theologian, ranked him with John the Divine.

And yet this venerable Christian practice—devoting one's life to stillness of mind, with clear explicit teaching from a master about how to achieve this—seems to have become increasingly rare over the last five centuries. There have been extraordinarily endowed individuals who attain the Kingdom of Heaven without benefit of a teacher, and there are still isolated monastic communities practicing some form of meditational prayer but these are only last vestiges of a robust tradition—the quivering flame of what was once a blazing fire.

But regarding solitary practitioners, the Fathers in the Egyptian desert advised that if you see someone climbing up the ladder to Heaven on his own, pull him back down. By this, the Desert Fathers seem to have meant that if you go it alone, without learning from the old men, you will not know how to learn—and moreover, you will not learn how to teach. It is through the learning process that one discovers what the beginner needs to know, and thus can pass it on. The rare case of the specially gifted person attaining realization on his or her own is an anomalous freak occurrence, and perishes without issue—sterile.

The transmission in Zen—and I suspect also in the early Orthodox and Celtic Churches—is not like this. "Anybody can be enlightened," Kyudo Roshi has said, "Give it three years."

Quite a mixed bag of people come to the London Zen Society, but all of them sincerely want to experience enlightenment. They are prepared to work for it, and also to suffer the pain that sitting often entails.

In Japanese monasteries, it is through at least three years of rigorous spiritual training that students are transformed into monks. "I don't know how," Kyudo Roshi says, "but it happens." The course is hard—but not impossibly so. There are two terms of just over three months each, three months and a week. This gives time for four seven-day sesshins, one at the beginning of the term, another at the end, and two in the middle, all a few weeks apart. In between terms, the monks can go home, where in many temples there is organized sitting for perhaps only half an hour per week. After three years, any who have stayed the course will have had some spiritual experience, and be sufficiently qualified to hold posts in temples elsewhere. They all know how to meditate—how to clear the mind and enter the pure state of *samadhi*—and they will have had a taste of the fruit of this work.

The organization of the Orthodox Christian Church and the Celtic Church was not unlike this. In the Orthodox Church, the bishops were drawn only from the ranks of the monks, so the social organization maintained some contact with the spiritual source and the practice of pure meditation. The dissemination of the practice in this way not only manifests its vitality, but also ensures its availability, and thereby helps it to survive.

Just as the viability of the academic life needs universities, libraries, and professors in order to survive, the life of pure meditation requires a certain organization to perpetuate its work and provide a framework in which the work can continue and thrive.

It is this that seems to have broken down in modern Christianity. Mainstream Christianity no longer teaches the necessary skills to meditate in the tradition of Jesus Christ. There is weighty evidence to suggest a line of transmission up to the end of the fourteenth century, and there are strong grounds for suspecting a break in this Christian transmission after that time—because it appears not to have reached us in this century.

An individual Christian master would shine like a living light, and a line of masters and their followers would blaze like a city of living flame for all to see. And yet Christians everywhere can look around and see no trace of this once-mighty fire. If a spiritual son cannot be born without a spiritual father, then such a lack would be final and irrevocable, a tragic loss of the living tradition of Christianity—if we remain confined to teachers in the Christian tradition only.

PART THREE
Christian Zen Practice

When seen in the broad sense, Zen means the Truth
or the Absolute: then it is not limited to Buddhism alone,
but is the basis of all religions and all philosophies.
For instance, there can be Christian Zen;
there can be Zen interpretations of Christianity.
Zen in the broadest sense should be understood and
used by all humanity because it can help build and refine
the character of the individual and can deepen thought.

Zenkei Shibayama Roshi, former Abbot of Nansenji, Kyoto

Zazen is not a difficult task. Just free yourself
from all incoming thoughts and hold your mind against them
like a great iron wall. Then some day you will meet
your true self as if you had awakened from a dream,
and will have the happiness you never could have
derived otherwise. Zen sitting is not a difficult task.
It is a way to lead you into your long-lost home.

Soen Shaku Zenji

7 CHRISTIAN ZEN PRACTICE

By Christian Zen practice, I do not mean anything different from doing *zazen* and going on *sesshin*—precisely the core of Zen Buddhist practice. Christian Zen practice is simply *zazen*, exactly as taught by the many spiritual generations of Zen teachers. Dogen Zenji, the thirteenth-century Japanese master who founded the Soto school of Zen, offers clear instructions for *zazen*:

> For *zazen* a quiet room is desirable and eating and drinking should be moderate. Stop the working and movement of the mind and empty the mind of all thoughts.
>
> Usually you put a thick covering on the floor where you sit and then put a round cushion on it. You may sit in the cross-legged or the half cross-legged position. In the former, you first put the right foot on the left thigh and then the left foot on the right thigh. In the latter, you only put the left foot on the right thigh. You must wear your clothes loosely but neatly. Next you must put the right hand on the left foot, and put the left palm in the right palm. The tips of the thumbs should lightly touch each other. Sit upright and do not incline to the left nor lean to the right. Do not stoop forward and do not throw back your head. The ears should be above the

shoulders and the nose in line with the navel. Place the tip of your tongue against the roof of your mouth. Lips should be together and so should the teeth. Eyes must always be open. Breath will pass gently through the nose and the body will be ready. Take a deep breath. Sway your body to right and left, and then sit firmly as a rock. Think of not thinking. How do we think of not thinking? By not thinking. This is the very basis of *zazen*.

Zazen is only serenity of mind. *Zazen* is the act of full enlightenment. The Truth is clearly recognized and now there exists no net and no cage. The true teaching appears by itself and all weariness and distraction fall away. When you get up, move your body slowly and stand up calmly; do not move violently.

It should be emphasized that Christian Zen practice is in no way radically different from pure meditation—pure contemplative prayer—as learned, practiced, and taught by the Desert Fathers who traced their lineage back to Christ. In fact, there was still a trace of this once central and dominant Christian tradition in England in the earlier part of this century as described by Abbot John Chapman of Downside, when superior of the community at Caldey in 1913:

[For contemplative prayer] the rules are extremely simple. St. John of the Cross has explained them, but a few notes founded on his teaching and on the experience of a number of people will possibly be useful.

Cease *all thinking* [his italics] and only make acts of will.

Let the acts come. They ought *not* to be fervent, but calm, simple, unmeaning, and unfelt. There are to be no feelings.

The essence of pure contemplative prayer is that these acts of will tend *always to be the same*.

It feels like the completest *waste of time*. The word "God" seems to mean nothing. Beware of trying to think what God is and what he has done for us, because this takes us out of prayer and spoils God's work, as St. John of the Cross says. Probably this is what St. Anthony meant, when he said *no one is praying really* if he knows what he is and what God is.

While the intellect is idle and empty, the will is fixed on God and remains united.

The real value of prayer can be securely estimated by its effect. It ought to produce very definite results:

All our spiritual life is unified into the one desire of union with God and His Will...

This prayer is easier when there is no noise, no distractions. The imagination has to be kept quiet. The night is generally a good time. The early morning perhaps best of all.

The most striking difference between the Zen Buddhist spiritual practice and the Christian practice is that the Zen Buddhists have continued to learn, practice, and teach their skills, while the Christians have not. I have learned *zazen* from living spiritual masters, sitting in the room with me, giving talks, interviewing me privately, and being my friends and companions; whereas I have only read about the Christian version. In no way at all could that reading have put me on the right track by itself. I needed a living teacher and a community to practice with.

Only when you have seen regular *zazen* and Zen retreats carried out with considerable preparations and great attention to detail— that is to say, only when you have seen it done right—do you come to realize how very easy it would be to get it wrong. And if you get the form wrong, you are not likely to attain the desired results.

Zen is, in essence, a science. The subject of the science is the living mind, which can be contacted at one point only, by sitting with it, facing the wall. The science is put into practice by abandoning thoughts engendered by centuries of conditioning, social indoctrination, and prejudice—and all imaginings. The aim of this science, as of any science, is to reach the rock bottom truth—reality. Kyudo Roshi calls this "the bottomless bottom." As in all science, attention to detail ensures the success or determines the failure of the investigation.

As I have shown, there are indications that meditating in a group was the original way of Christian practice, and that this may have been what Jesus Christ's followers were doing when He appeared to them after the resurrection—and was certainly what they were doing "persevering in meditation" when they were transformed by the Spirit at Pentecost. But meditating in a group is a practice that has been neglected among Christians.

On Zen retreats, although each individual is left to a personal struggle—his or her own particular hermitage, isolated on the mat, with the patch of blank wall for a cave—the individual nevertheless gets great strength and support from those others practicing there. This community strength immensely increases the strength and determination of the individual. It is a very recognizable fact that you can do much more in a group than on your own, especially in the first stages of practice. An hour of sitting with a group is more manageable than half an hour alone at home.

Zen teachers talk quite often about how you will make compromises when you try to practice on your own. As you are not disturbing anyone else, you don't mind shifting position to get a bit more comfortable—and then shifting again. You may cut the sitting short, then a bit shorter—and end up by not sitting at all. But it is your own sitting that you disturb by moving, destroying the effort you've made up until then, by stirring up the mind and ego. It is yourself that you cheat of sitting time.

It is as if psychological work were exactly like heavy physical work; whereas alone you could never get that large boulder up the hill, with ten people all pushing together, you can.

The Still Body Stills the Mind

When sitting in the Zen position (after a precarious and wobbly start) you will eventually come to feel like a tower of stability, built firmly on foundations of rock. As a Christian, this feeling reminds me of Christ's words:

> Why do you call me Lord, and not do what I say? Anyone who listens to my words and acts accordingly—shall I give you an idea of what he is like? He is like a man who in building a house, dug and went deep and laid his foundations on the rock; so that when the river rose in flood and beat against the house, it was not strong enough to shake it for it was well-built.

Abbot Isaac of the Desert echoes this idea:

> The aim of every monk and the perfection of his heart tends to continual and unbroken perseverance in meditation and strives to acquire immovable tranquillity of mind and a perpetual purity. Our unwearied and constant practice is laid on strong foundations, that rock of the Gospel, and by being built in this way, this tower will rise to the utmost heights of heaven in full assurance of its stability. And therefore in order that meditation may be earnest and pure as it ought, we must by all means observe these rules.

It is remaining still for long hours that continues to settle the mind; if you keep stirring it, then it will never settle.

A seven-day Zen retreat is the main event in Zen, and all regular or daily sitting is to some extent a preparation for, or continuation of, this main event. A form of meditation that might be adequate for one hour of sitting, but not for a whole day of sitting, is inadequate because it cannot be maintained. At first, as you are getting used to the Zen way of sitting, it may seem quite difficult but only after a Zen retreat can the value of the *zazen* posture be fully appreciated.

Stability is the base of stillness, and the Zen position is the most stable that the human body can get into. Just as a tripod is used for holding a camera still, so the Zen position rests on three points: the buttocks and the two knees. Ideally this is achieved by getting into the full-lotus or half-lotus position, as described by Dogen. But some Westerners cannot do this. Every single Zen teacher and Zen monk has sat in this position—except one: the great Daito Zenji (1282–1338), who at one time was the teacher of the Japanese Emperor. The reason he could not manage the lotus position was because he was crippled. It is said that he pulled his crippled leg into the full-lotus position only once in his life—when he was dying.

Even when you are experienced, it is much harder to get into *samadhi* (the state of pure mind) while lying down. It is easier standing up, but that position is difficult to endure long. Perhaps with a sword as third foot (like the Christian knights standing in vigil before the altar to prepare for the day of battle) it might be possible. But by far the steadiest and most stable position is cross-legged on the floor, with the knees on the mat and the buttocks on the cushion. But it's no use tying your legs in fancy knots if it does not result is a good solid base. Some Westerners can only achieve this solid base in a kneeling position (*seiza*) with their bottom on the cushions, which are sometimes turned sideways, and the knees at least two fists apart. Special benches, called *seiza* benches, are made to facilitate sitting in this position. It is better to sit solidly on a chair or a *seiza* bench than to keep shifting and wobbling on Zen cushions.

Kyudo Roshi once said that if you want to transform your mind then you must do something different. If you do the same things all the time, then you stay the same. If you sit about on a chair all day and then come to Zen and sit about on a chair, your mind is all too likely to trundle along in the same old ruts: You are unlikely to attain the pure, empty mind—let alone enlightenment.

The traditional Zen cushion, called a *zafu*, has one open pleat around the side so that you can stuff in more filling (or take some out) according to need. All kinds of circumstances affect this need, from a twisted ankle to a sore back. It is important to arrange the cushions carefully and take up a good, solid position—and then to keep to it, usually for half an hour at a stretch in the *zendo*, and preferably for a similar period at home.

The solid triangular base is what gives maximum support to the back. Even if you are not limber, your back still gets necessary support when you sit cross-legged with your feet on the floor, or in the quarter-lotus position with one leg propped on the calf of the other leg. But if you are more supple, then it is a valuable help to lock the back by bringing up the legs onto the thighs close to the groin. The major disadvantage of placing both feet on the mat (in what is called the modified Burmese position) is that you are forced to do the splits more, and there is more tension between the calf muscles and the thigh muscles, which can add to the general discomfort, but it works well enough nonetheless. In any event, some regular stretching exercises can help make any position more comfortable.

If the back is absolutely straight, and the nose is in line with the navel, the body holds still with a minimum of muscular effort. The elongated position of the back helps to lengthen the breath, which in turn calms the mind.

The hands should be placed in the lap, one hand resting on the other. The thumbs are lifted to form an oval, with the tips just touching lightly. This hand position is a great aid to concentration: when you lose concentration the thumbs flop, and this helps to recall your attention to the breath. On the other extreme, pressing too hard indicates too much tension, which leads to exhaustion.

Most Christians pray with their eyes shut, but this has two major disadvantages: either you doze off, or you get caught up in the inner world of thought and imagination—watching your personal TV set, as Kyudo Roshi calls it. In *zazen*, you look straight ahead and then drop your eyelids, which diffuses your vision a bit, as if you were looking through a soft gauze curtain. In this way, you are shielded from the outside world, which is veiled in a soft light, but at the same time you are not thrown into the even more turbulent and noisy inner world of the imagination.

In *zazen*, the back is to be like a steel bolt—or an arrow to heaven—and the rest of the body is relaxed. The shoulders are relaxed, the cheeks are relaxed, the mouth is shut but not clenched tight. The tongue rests lightly on the roof of the mouth to minimize the need for swallowing. Of course, some involuntary swallowing is inevitable. Totally involuntary movements (such as stomach rumblings or swallowing) do not disturb sitting, but any conscious movement defeats the purpose and nullifies the effort.

The whole point of *zazen* is stillness. Christian meditation recognizes the centrality of stillness as well: One word used for monks and hermits, *hesychast,* means "one who is still." Sometimes these monks took up position in meditation as the sun set behind them and did not budge till the sun rose in front of them.

Dissolving the Mind into the Breath

There is a tradition in Christianity of uniting a simple prayer (or even just the name of Jesus) with the breath. Knowledge of this practice filtered into the West through the popular *Way of a Pilgrim* by an anonymous Russian Orthodox man who ended his days as a monk on Mount Athos. I once met a German Jesuit who practiced this by dividing the name of Jesus (in German, *Jesu*) into the two syllables—*JE* and *SU*—and uniting *JE* with his incoming breath and *SU* with the outgoing breath

Experiencing the perfection of God is possible for the Christian only if his ego is dissolved into the living spirit of God through pure meditation—and the practice of just breathing. The breath, for the Christian, is thus related to the Holy Spirit, the breath of Life.

In due course, during meditation the head itself becomes physically cool and the mind pure, while the lower belly generates heat to the lower limbs. It is a very natural state. Pure existence, pure life, pure mind—these three are one.

In the catechism that I was brought up on, we learned by heart and recited in unison: "What is prayer? Prayer is the raising of the mind and heart to God." We were all supposed to do it, but unfortunately the instructions about *how* to do it were missing. So some people, like me, wasted a bit of time vaguely imagining themselves raised into the presence of God—whereas in fact they had only taken the much shorter step into the back room of their imagination.

Just sitting. Just breathing.

Yet this simple activity is in fact quite a physical effort, especially in the context of a *sesshin*. Nobody who has not done it would ever be able to guess what a sport it is. No mere spectator of the sport could ever know how strenuous it is. I had been a skillful boxer, had trained for athletics, and had played wing on the school rugby team, but I was still surprised when I encountered the arduous physical training of Zen. Some people who have reached a certain accomplishment in the martial arts will confirm that a Zen retreat is harder. But as physically challenging as a Zen retreat is, one must not underestimate the mental challenges.

Sometimes it feels as if each period of Zen sitting is a round of battle, and a Zen *sesshin* a war. The fierce battle is against one's own stubborn ego. Sitting in *zazen*, period after period, gives you front row seats as your ego struggles impossibly against itself.

"Big ego—take it out," Sochu Roshi used to say. "Empty. Shining empty dustbins. All golden dustbins." He pointed at each one of us: "You—golden dustbin."

Once when I went for my private interview I asked him if the ego was good for anything at all? "Of course," he said. "Use it—use it to fight stubborn ego."

Christians brought up on the teaching of self-denial will immediately see the point of striking the ego on its home ground, rather than by beating about the bush depriving it of buns in Lent—which can all too easily provide just the kind of satisfaction and gratification the ego is looking for.

The battle begins with the simple maneuver of just sitting still and silent. This is a practice wholly repellent to the ego—as a person who sits down to do *zazen* for the first time will immediately see.

That is round one—and it is surprising how difficult round one is. The ego wins when we shift position, scratch an itch, look around, give in to our imagination—any of these actions nullifies our *zazen*. Yet the battle *can* be won—and attention to the breath is the key.

Calm breathing gradually calms the mind.

The mind at one with calm breathing ignores, dismisses, and slowly dissolves thoughts.

Yet be wary—just when you begin to get some control of your thoughts, then the imagination starts playing up. "You just sit there watching your inner TV set. That's not *zazen*," Kyudo Roshi would say. You have to notice and dissolve the images. What's left? Nothing—and now the ego gets frantic at the prospect of dissolving. It makes one last whining appeal: You are overwhelmed with the feeling that you must move to relieve your pain; you must wipe the snot trickling from your nostril; you must clear your throat; you must scratch an itch. But if you can keep going—ignoring such tricks of the ego—you will get into deeper meditation soon after. Plunging deeper into meditation is the only way of ignoring these plaintive calls. It is very often just after resisting such distractions that you reach your goal of *samadhi*.

Just concentrate all your attention on your breath. Your calm, steady breathing calms and steadies the mind. And the calm mind further calms the breathing.

The ego simply detests this process. It longs to pant, to move, to think, to imagine. It clutches at any and all of these, given the slightest chance—with manic tenacity. And prizing the grip of ego-attachment loose is not easy.

All of this is wholly compatible with Christian ideals—and never more so than in the next stage of meditation, when the battle with the ego becomes a battle to the death.

"Die on your mat," is the consistent Zen teaching.

And there you sit—still as a corpse, silent as the dead—extinguishing all thoughts, putting out all imaginings, like lights, until you yourself go out like a light. For a Christian, this is surely related to dying daily with Christ.

This death is the necessary precondition to waking up to the indestructible living force that is the very working order of the universe. This is the intangible, invisible essential nature of the universe. It is closely related to traditional Christian teaching about the Holy Spirit—discoverable in the depths of the soul, and at work throughout nature. This is the very experience of reality as it is—simple, basic, apparent to those who have sat in meditation until it manifests itself. Then it is undeniable. As Kyudo Roshi said, "You can't be wrong about reality."

The surprising thing is that we could have missed it before—somehow failing to notice the nature of our own living experience. The working order of the universe is extraordinary. The same working order activating or animating me and it, together, as one entity. You might call this working order the universal law, the natural order, the Way of Heaven and Earth, or the Kingdom of Heaven. And you would not be wrong. But you might prefer not to give it a name for fear people might confuse the name, and their associations around the name, with the realization itself.

In *A Bodhisattva's Vow*, Torei Zenji comments on what follows from the realization of this reality:

> This realization made our patriarchs and virtuous Zen masters extend tender care, with the heart of worshipping to such beings as beasts and birds. Who can be ungrateful or not respectful even to senseless things, not to speak of men?

Suitable Circumstances

It is very important to search out or create suitable circumstances for practicing *zazen*. As Dogen said, find a quiet place. Outside noises can be distracting in the early stages of practice, external quiet helps foster inner silence. The Desert Fathers knew this. There is a story of a young monk who had set up his hermitage near the river. One of the old men told the young monk that he could not possibly meditate with all that racket of the wind rustling in the reeds; so the monk moved deeper into the silence of the desert's interior.

Zen monks traditionally sought out remote spots and engineered everything in a way that was most conducive to *zazen*, so that the world around them was at one with the living individual—the immaculately clean room where they sat, the clean bowls from which they ate—all this helped to clear the mind. Their *zazen* was reflected in the stone garden, and the stone garden was reflected in their rocklike sitting in *zazen*.

However, one should not get hung up on seeking ideal circumstances in which to meditate. It is equally important to be able to do *zazen* and attain *samadhi* under any circumstances whatsoever.

Right from the start, you are looking both for perfection in every detail and for making use of everything apparently adverse. One Zen master said that meditation has not been perfected until you can sit in the middle of the busiest bridge in Kyoto as if you were in the silent depths of a great forest.

Under adverse circumstances (which are inevitable), if you can manage to sit in spite of the difficulty, your sitting cannot help but gain in strength. In order to continue to meditate, you are forced to try harder, and this, in itself, is beneficial. Many who have done *zazen* may have experienced how they only really began to get the hang of it when they were forced to deal with some potential distraction: a terrible itch or a fly crawling over the face or a running nose or the sound of a passing car. There is a technique of entering the noise, vibrating with it outward to the place where the noise dies away, the place where the noise no longer penetrates.

This technique can be applied to every other potentially distracting circumstance. Of course it is advisable to get a good Zen mat and Zen cushion; but if you can do *zazen* on a blanket folded in four and pillow doubled over, then you will be able to continue in every circumstance—even in a hotel room, even in a prison. I once heard a story of a person using a public bathroom as the private spot he needed with just enough space to meditate—but he had not reckoned on the cleaning lady with her master key. Seeing him, she immediately backed away bowing, as if it were her mistake, that she had burst in on a holy shrine!

Above all, it is a great advantage to practice in a group—especially at first, especially if the group is made up mostly of experienced sitters, and even more especially if there is a Zen master in charge, and most especially when he is sitting in the room with you. But if there is no such group available, consider this: There is a belief that the teacher and the group will somehow materialize if the efforts you make on your own are sufficiently sincere. It is said that "When the student is ready, the teacher will appear."

8 WHAT COMES NEXT?

How much time must one spend meditating? How often must one go on a Zen retreat? Just one *sesshin*, and the individual is no longer confused about the point of sitting: he or she knows where it is leading and has a sense where it would lead with more effort. I have not yet met the person who regretted having gone on a Zen retreat—at least once it was over. Kyudo Roshi said that his novices in Japan were different after they had done the hard winter *Rohatsu sesshin*. I am inclined to think that those people who have done even one *sesshin* will remember it on their deathbed.

There is nothing in modern Christian practice to compare with it. I am confident that if a *sesshin* became one of those things that people did only once in a lifetime—like the old pilgrimages or the journey to Mecca—it would still have an extraordinary effect on the spiritual life of a society, or even a community within that society.

A seven-day *sesshin* is crucial because the mind takes about three days to settle, and this affects the quality of the *zazen* dramatically. After that, every hour of sitting is easier, goes by faster, and is far more valuable—one hour on the fourth day is the equivalent of a whole day at the beginning of the retreat.

The most difficult thing about *sesshin* is getting yourself there in the first place. The ego makes it hard to begin a retreat, as if it senses the danger to itself that is ahead, and it strives to avoid even entering the first round of the battle—which may entail losing the war of ego-centered survival. Once you are there and the retreat is under way, it has its own compelling charm. But like the benefits, the pain and the hard effort required are also cumulative—as if you were trying to scale an increasingly precipitous mountain for the first three days. Nevertheless few people drop out once they have got there.The preparation, the clothing, the equipment are all important. As with climbing a mountain, an experienced guide can lead a few inexperienced people through the climb.

At the London Zen Society the resident priest often holds weekend *sesshins*, which are valuable at least for getting to know the ropes. However, in a shorter *sesshin* one may not experience the dramatic change in the quality of sitting that often takes place around the third or fourth day. The weekend *sesshin*, from Friday night to Sunday (arranged more to fit in with people's work schedules than for reasons to do with Zen) is a valuable preparation for a longer sesshin. It also offers a glimpse of the impact of returning from *sesshin* to everyday life—which may be fraught with difficulties—but is nevertheless a real experience of the relationship between spiritual practice and daily life.

But bear this in mind: In order to attain enlightenment, the Buddha devoted six years to spiritual training, and Bodhidharma spent nine years facing a wall. This seems to be a clue to the magnitude of devotion required for such an attainment.

For Christians, each of us must begin by combining a few prolonged bursts of effort, in the form of retreats, with some amount of steady, daily sitting if we are ever to establish a tradition of Christian Zen practice. An hour's regular sitting every day, or perhaps even a half-hour, and two Zen retreats a year might be just enough to bring about the beginnings of a return to the old Christian tradition. But it would depend on restoring a link, via Zen, in the chain of spiritual masters. Nevertheless, I am convinced there are many Christians who—once the way ahead is illuminated—will be capable of following it, and thereby will restore Christianity to what it once was.

Reality is like a priceless jewel, of which the most priceless diamond is only an inadequate metaphor. Once the tar has been scraped away by *sesshin*—layer after layer, *zazen* period after *zazen* period—then the jewel reveals itself. And we will see the freedom of this universe of pure existence, just as it is—the Kingdom of Heaven.

RECOMMENDED READING LIST

Zen Books

DOGEN
Shobogenzo, 13th Century
(English translation by Gudo Nishijima and Chodo Cross published by
Windbell in 1994–99)
A masterpiece of spiritual writing, full of marvelous insights, but dense and
somewhat obscure at times. Rediscovered in 1910 after centuries of neglect.
For the importance of *zazen*, see especially chapters 1, 27, 58 and 72.

HAKUIN
The Embossed Tea Kettle, 18th Century
(English translation by R.D.M. Shaw published by George Allen and
Unwin in 1963)
Includes an exhortation to do *zazen*; even more inspiring than his *Song
of Zazen*.

HUI NENG
The Sutra of Hui Neng, 7th Century.
(English translation reissued by Shambhala Publications in 1990)
This text is also known as the *The Platform Sutra* of the Sixth Zen Patriarch.
With *The Zen Teaching of Huang Po* (Jap. *Obaku*) *on the Transmission of Mind*,
and Hui Hai (Jap. *Hyakujo*) *Zen Teaching of Instantaneous Awakening* (English
translation by John Blofeld) these three present a clear, concise account of
the teaching of the founding patriarchs of Zen in China. Each includes a
marvelous short verse summing up the whole of their teaching.

KAPLEAU, Philip
The Three Pillars of Zen
(Published by Beacon Press in 1967)

The valuable material gathered has led to a widespread interest in Zen practice: it includes an account of Harada Roshi, Yasutani Roshi's introductory lectures on Zen, and what was for me the first *teisho* in English (on the *koan Mu*), plus an interesting collection of modern enlightenment experiences.

SAHN, Seung
Dropping Ashes on the Buddha
(Published by Grove Press in 1976)
Pithy, convincing teaching of a Korean Zen master in America.

SEKIDA, Katsuki
Zen Training
(Published by Weatherhill in 1975)
If it were possible to learn to meditate from a book, this would surely be the book. But I have to say I tried in 1974—when the book was still in manuscript—and failed. But the book did help me enormously once I joined a group. Sekida helped with Sochu Roshi's London group as well as Aitken Roshi's group in Hawaii, so he is aware of Western problems, mentality, etc.

SHIBAYAMA, Zenkei
Zen Comments on the Mumonkan
(English translation by Sumiko Kudo published by Harper and Row in 1974)
The key collection of *koans* with a commentary that brings to life the story of Zen in China with its array of astonishing masters through seven centuries. See also Shibayama's *A Flower Does Not Talk* for his ideas about the verse attributed to Bodhidharma on transmission outside the scriptures, direct mind to mind.

SOKEI-AN
The Zen Eye
(Published by Weatherhill in 1993)
A follower of Soen Shaku Roshi, Sokei-an was highly influential in the early stages of introducing Zen to the West. These are beautifully edited versions of his delightful talks to his small New York groups. Especially good on the traditional Five Eyes of Buddhism.

SUZUKI, Daisetz Teitaro

The Training of a Zen Buddhist Monk

(Published by The Eastern Buddhist Society in 1934, and later reissued by Globe Press Books)

The earliest account in English of Zen practice that I know of; short and still worth reading. It could well be prefaced by Jung's introduction to another D.T. Suzuki book, in which Jung believes it impossible for Zen to catch on in the West: either he was wrong, or, as I prefer to think, Zen teachers in the West are achieving the impossible.

SUZUKI, Shunryu

Zen Mind, Beginner's Mind

(Published by Weatherhill in 1970)

Shunryu Suzuki is not to be confused with Sochu Suzuki, my teacher, or Daisetz Suzuki, mentioned above. This book is among the best introductory books for the practice of Zen.

Christian Books

ATTWATER, D.

Dictionary of Saints (Revised version)

(Published by Penguin Books in 1979)

A good entry on St. Josaphat (The Buddha), but also includes many of the Orthodox saints (who are not well enough known in the West), for example, Anthony of the Caves, who brought Christian monasticism from the Mount Athos region to Russia.

BUDGE, E.A. Wallis

English translation of *The Wit and Wisdom of the Christian Fathers of Egypt*

(Published by Oxford University Press in 1934)

Also *The Paradise of the Fathers* (Published by Chatto and Windus in 1907), which includes the Life of St. Anthony. Wonderful glimpses of men and women who turned one of the most inhospitable regions on earth into a much sought-after paradise.

CASSIAN, John
Institutes and *Conferences*
(Edited by Henry Wace and James Parker, and published by Oxford University Press in 1894)
His aim is to instruct the spiritually minded to attain the perfect life by means of the rules and customs observed since the rise of the apostolic age.

CHAPMAN, John
The Spiritual Letters
(Published by Sheed and Ward in 1935)
See especially pp. 287–94: *Contemplative Prayer, a few simple rules.*

CLOUD OF UNKNOWING
Anonymous
(Published by Burns Oats in 1924)
This edition includes the translation of the *Hidden Divinity* by Denys, and Augustine Baker's comment on "Nothing and nothing make nothing." But the best modern English version is by Clifton Wolters (Penguin Books 1961).

LOSSKY, Vladimir
Mystical Theology of the Eastern Church
(Reissued in 1991 by James Clarke)
The profound psychology of the Orthodox masters is very striking.

MEYENDORFF, John
A Study of Gregory of Palamas
(Published by Faith Press in 1964)
An account from the Eastern standpoint of a key episode in the story of Christian meditation as practiced by the Orthodox monks (the *hesychasts*), which stressed, above all, stillness, but also following the breath. It was condemned briefly for its resemblance to meditation-yoga (that is, *dhyana* or Zen!), but Palamas showed it was pure Christian contemplative prayer, as practiced since the time of the Apostles. He was vindicated in his life-time, drew up his "Declaration in defense of those who practice the life of stillness," and was canonized and made Doctor (Teacher) of the Orthodox faith.

PHILOKALIA, The
Compiled by St. Nikodemus of the Holy Mountain and St. Makarios of
Corinth.
(English translation by G.E.H. Palmer, et al., published by Faber and Faber
1979–99)
For those Christians pursuing the path of spiritual perfection, this anthol-
ogy of the Christian spiritual masters is ranked second only to the Bible.
The Way of a Pilgrim tells the delightful tale of an anonymous Russian on his
way to Mount Athos. See especially the texts on prayer and watchfulness.
(This is the source of quotations in the present text from the following:
Denys, Evagrios the Solitary, John Cassian, St. Hesychios, St. Maximos,
Simeon the New Theoligian, St. Philotheos, and St. Gregory of Palamas.)

RIEU, E.V.
Translation of *The Four Gospels*
(Published by Penguin Books in 1952)
Rieu's great learning (he also translated Homer and edited Penguin
Classics) is admirably concealed in the art of his lively style, which
brought out for me the humanity of Christ—"like us in everything but
sin." If so, he would need spiritual teachers, suggested by the story of his
meeting with such teachers in the Temple around the age of twelve.

SMITH, Morton
The Secret Gospel
(Published by Aquarian Press in 1973)
Somewhat deceptively subtitled *The Discovery and Interpretation of the Secret
Gospel according to Mark*, whereas there is only a brief mention and short
extract of such a Gospel—but it does open vistas of possibilities. More
important is that Christ appears to initiate a young follower into the mystery of the Kingdom of Heaven; after six days and a night of vigil, and possibly involving a symbolic death.

The East/West Dialogue

AMORE, Roy C.
Two Masters, One Message: The Lives and Teachings of Gautama and Jesus
(Published by Abingdon Press in 1978)
Suggests that Buddhism and Christianity are twin expressions of one wide-spread spiritual movement. Jerusalem is nearer to India than to London or Madrid, and there were many occasions for contact.

BLYTH, R.H.
Zen in English Literature
(Published by Hokuseido Press in 1942)
Did much to whet the appetite of the Western reader for Zen books, an interest further aroused by Paul Reps and Eugene Herrigel. Blyth also wrote *Buddhist Sermons on Christian Texts*.

BROSSE, Jacques
Les Maitres Spirituels
(Published by Bordas in 1988)
Somewhat in the vein of such pioneer works as F.C. Happold's *Mysticism*, and Aldous Huxley's *Perennial Philosophy*, Brosse outlines the main figures and movements of the great world religions, rarely more than a page or two for each. Concise but well done with quotes and references. He includes Jung. No English translation yet. See also his *Satori dix ans d'expe-rience avec un maitre Zen*.

GRAHAM, Dom Aelred (OSB)
Zen Catholicism
(Published by Collins in 1964)
An early milestone in the Zen-Christian dialogue by the prior of the Bene-dictine community in Portsmouth, Rhode Island.

HABITO, Ruben
Total Liberation
(Published by Orbis in 1989)
Probably the best book to date on Christianity transformed by Zen.

JÄGER, Willigis (OSB)
Contemplation, a Christian Path
(Published by Ligouri in 1994)
A Christian Path, but rediscovered through Zen: he is a *roshi* in the *Sanbo Kyodan* school of Zen, with hundreds of followers in Germany. He is also a Benedictine monk.

JOHNSTON, William (SJ)
Silent Music
(Published by Collins in 1974)
Expresses growing Catholic interest in Zen spirituality and the sound reasons for it. A Jesuit priest who also wrote *The Still Point: Reflections on Zen and Christian Mysticism*, and *Christian Zen*. For a Jesuit colleague also involved in the practice and teaching of Zen, see Robert E. Kennedy, *Zen Spirit, Christian Spirit* (Published by Continuum in 1995).

LASSALLE, Hugo Enomiya (SJ)
Zen Meditation for Christians
(English translation by John C. Maraldo published by Open Court in 1974)
His major work comparing Zen with Christian contemplatives such as Richard of St. Victor, who influenced the author of *The Cloud of Unknowing*, as well as Dante. See also his *Zen: The Way to Enlightenment*.

MACINNES, Elaine (Our Lady's Missionaries)
Light Sitting in Light
(Published by HarperCollins in 1996)
These are introductory talks for beginners by a Catholic missionary nun. See also *Comments on the Mumonkan*, by Yamada Koun Roshi, her teacher.

SUZUKI, Daisetz T.
Mysticism Christian and Buddhist
(Published by George Allen and Unwin in 1957)
Another milestone in the Zen-Christian dialogue, but this time from the Buddhist standpoint. Also from the Buddhist base is Thich Nhat Hanh's *Living Buddha, Living Christ*, (Published by Riverhead in 1997) and the Dalai Lama's *The Good Heart* (published by Wisdom Publications in 1997).

ABOUT THE AUTHOR

Born to agnostic parents, Tom Chetwynd converted to Catholicism while attending a boarding school run by Benedictine monks. For the last twenty-five years, he has endeavored to combine his Christian and Zen practices, and since 1982, he has taught Zen meditation in London with the approval of Sochu Roshi of Ryutakuji Monastery in Japan. He leads evening sitting groups, weekend retreats, and, for the last ten years, annual week-long *sesshins*. He has also held workshops and taught meditation in prisons throughout England. His other published works include *The Dictionary for Dreamers, The Dictionary of Symbols,* and *How to Interpret Your Own Dreams.*

ALSO FROM WISDOM PUBLICATIONS

THE GOOD HEART:
A Buddhist Perspective on the Teachings of Jesus
The Dalai Lama
Paper, ISBN 0-86171-138-6, $14.95; Clothbound, ISBN 0-86171-114-9, $24.00

The Dalai Lama provides an extraordinary Buddhist perspective on the teachings of Jesus, commenting on well-known passages from the four Christian Gospels including the Sermon on the Mount, the parable of the mustard seed, the Resurrection, and others.

"Sparkling wit and compassionate understanding mark these penetrating insights of the Dalai Lama into spiritual foundations of two of the world's great religious traditions. Highly recommended." —*Library Journal*

THE FINE ARTS OF RELAXATION,
CONCENTRATION AND MEDITATION:
Ancient Skills for Modern Minds
Joel & Michelle Levey
Paper, ISBN 0-86171-040-1, $14.95

"Practical and down-to-earth, this is a remarkable and comprehensive workbook for mastering the stress of life." —NAPRA ReVIEW

"The methods included here work wonders. As a satisfied user of so many of them, I affirm that they truly deepen the appreciation of life."
—*Ram Dass, author of* Be Here Now *and* Still Here:
Embracing Aging, Changing, and Dying

MINDFULNESS IN PLAIN ENGLISH
Bhante Henepola Gunaratana
Paper, ISBN 0-86171-064-9, $14.95

This step-by-step guide to Insight Meditation is truly practical and direct.

Venerable Gunaratana's conversational style and use of everyday examples imbue the basic teachings of meditation with unsurpassable clarity and wit. His deeply spiritual yet nondenominational approach invites readers of all backgrounds to experience and enjoy the fruits of meditative awareness.

"One of the best nuts-and-bolts meditation manuals. If you'd like to learn the practice of meditation, you can't do better."
—*Amazon.com Delivers Eastern Religion*

"A masterpiece. I cannot recommend it highly enough."
—*Jon Kabat-Zinn, author of* Wherever You Go, There You Are

HOW TO MEDITATE
A Practical Guide
Kathleen McDonald
Paper, ISBN 0-86171-009-6, $14.95

What is meditation? Why practice it? How do I do it? The answers to these often-asked questions are contained in this down-to-earth book written by a Western Buddhist nun with solid experience in both the practice and teaching of meditation.

"This book is as beautifully simple and direct as its title." —*Yoga Today*

"Simple, direct, and complete." —*Wisconsin Bookwatch*

IMAGINE ALL THE PEOPLE:
A Conversation with the Dalai Lama on Money, Politics, and Life as it Could Be
The Dalai Lama with Fabien Ouaki
Paper, ISBN 0-86171-150-5, $14.95

The Dalai Lama, through conversation with prominent French businessman Fabien Ouaki, offers his unique perspective on the issues of today: money and the economy, the environment, disarmament, and basic human ethics. Blessed by His Holiness' buoyant and insightful thoughts, *Imagine All the People* allows readers to glimpse the spontaneous workings of an extraordinary mind.

ABOUT WISDOM

Wisdom Publications, a not-for-profit publisher, is dedicated to making available authentic Buddhist works for the benefit of all. We publish translations of the sutras and tantras, commentaries and teachings of past and contemporary Buddhist masters, and original works by the world's leading Buddhist scholars. We publish our titles with the appreciation of Buddhism as a living philosophy and with the special commitment to preserve and transmit important works from all the major Buddhist traditions.

If you would like more information or a copy of our mail-order catalog, please contact us at:

Wisdom Publications
199 Elm Street
Somerville, Massachusetts 02144 USA
Telephone: (617) 776-7416 • Fax: (617) 776-7841
Email: sales@wisdompubs.org • www.wisdompubs.org

THE WISDOM TRUST

As a not-for-profit publisher, Wisdom Publications is dedicated to the publication of fine Dharma books for the benefit of all sentient beings and dependent upon the kindness and generosity of sponsors in order to do so. If you would like to make a donation to Wisdom, please do so through our Somerville office. If you would like to sponsor the publication of a book, please write or e-mail us for more information.

Thank you.

Wisdom Publications is a non-profit, charitable 501(c)(3) organization affiliated with the Foundation for the Preservation of the Mahayana Tradition (FPMT).